CHARLESTON SOUTH CAROLINA

RESIDENTS

1782-1794

❧❦

Carroll Ainsworth McElligott

Heritage Books
2025

HERITAGE BOOKS

AN IMPRINT OF HERITAGE BOOKS, INC.

Books, CDs, and more—Worldwide

For our listing of thousands of titles see our website
at
www.HeritageBooks.com

A Facsimile Reprint
Published 2025 by
HERITAGE BOOKS, INC.
Publishing Division
5810 Ruatan Street
Berwyn Heights, MD 20740

International Standard Book Number
Paperbound: 978-1-55613-255-1

Table of Contents

Introduction

The purpose of this book is to provide an account of the residents of Charleston, South Carolina, during the period 1782 through 1794. The source for this study is the extant Charleston City Directories for that period.

Prior to the Revolutionary War, Charleston had a distinct English flavor and reflected the tastes of eighteenth century England. Virtually all business that South Carolinians and residents of the neighboring provinces had with Great Britain was conducted through Charleston prior to the Revolutinary War.

The Revolutionary War brought about great changes in Charleston. Merchants, craftsmen, teachers, ministers, and others who were loyal to the King had fled or had been exiled. Charleston had severed her ties with England and had become an American city. By 1790 Charleston had recovered from the destruction of the war and from the economic chaos which was brought about by the severing of business ties with Great Britain. These changes are evident in the growth of the city and in the occupational trends which are reflected in this study.

The following city directories have been consulted for this study:

   The South Carolina and Georgia Almanack, for the year of our Lord 1782; Being second, after LEAP-YEAR. CONTAINING The Lunations; Eclipses; Rising and Setting of the Moon and Stars; Aspects; Judgment of the Weather; &c. &c. &c. by John Tobler, Esq. (Charlestown: Printed by R. Wells & Son, and Sold at their Stationary, Musick & Book Store, No. 71, Tradd Street; and in Georgia, by Mr. David Zubly in Savannah).

   The South Carolina and Georgia Almanack for 1785, by John Tobler. (Issued in 1784.)

   The Charleston Directory; and Revenue System of the United States. By Jacob Milligan. (Charleston: Printed by T. B. Bowen, 1790).

   The Charleston Directory by Jacob Milligan, Harbour Master. (Charleston: Printed by W. P. Young, September, 1794).

The 1782 Charleston City Directory was the first printed directory for any American city or town, although it was not printed in separate form.

Microfilm copies of these directories are available at the Charleston Public Library, Meeting Street, Charleston, South Carolina, and at the Charleston Library Society, King Street, Charleston, South Carolina.

This study, except for the 1785 directory, has been divided by the occupations of the residents and then subdivided according to the year. Each chapter, except the last one, consists of two parts - an introductory essay and a listing of the residents whose occupation is included in the category which is covered by the chapter. If an individual is listed as having two occupations, such as printer and stationer, he is included in the chapter "Craftsmen" as a printer and in the chapter "Mercantile Community" as a stationer.

The last chapter concerns the 1785 directory. Since the 1785 directory listed only the names and addresses of most of the residents, a different format has been devised for this directory. The names of the 1785 residents are listed in alphabetical order. The address is included if it is listed in the 1785 directory. The information regarding occupation which is included in the 1785 directory is included. Information regarding the occupation of some residents has been obtained from other sources. The source of the information is included in the entry.

All entries of name, occupation, and address follow the spelling and punctuation of the original entry. The reader is reminded that, although the directories were typeset, it is often difficult to distinguish between "f" and "s" since both usually appear as "f" in these directories. The glossary includes definitions of eighteenth century occupations based largely on eighteenth and nineteenth century sources. There is a full-name index. Abbreviations, spellings, and titles which appear in the original entries have been retained in the index.

Carroll Ainsworth McElligott

Harleyville, South Carolina
May, 1988

Chapter I / Craftsmen

Craftsman is defined as one who practices some trade or manual occupation.

During the late eighteenth century Charleston was a major seaport and shipbuilding center. This is evident in the number of craftsmen who were skilled in the various phases of ship construction.

Stonecutters were responsible for the carved tombstones of the post-Revolutionary period which are still standing in South Carolina graveyards today. Many of these stonecutters carved marble chimney pieces also.

There was a considerable number of painters in Charleston in the late eighteenth century. Many of these worked as portrait painters as well as painted buildings, taught art lessons, etc.

In the 1790's the cessation of building which occurred during and immediately following the Revolutionary War ended. The 1790's reflect a considerable increase in the number of craftsmen in such areas as carpenters, bricklayers, cabinet makers, etc.

Charleston had the same kind of craftsmen, such as tanner, watchmaker, seamstress, taylor, silversmith, etc., as were found in any major city during the latter part of the eighteenth century.

A count of the craftsmen is shown below.

Craftsmen

	1782	1790	1794
baker	4	31	22
band box mak.		1	
barber	1	1	10
blacksmith	2	16	13
blockmaker		2	3
bookbinder	1	2	2

	1782	1790	1794
brass founder		1	1
brewer	1	2	
bricklayer		19	12
brickmaker		1	2
butcher		30	22
button maker		1	
cabinet maker	1	15	16
cake maker			1
carpenter	5	68	69
carter		9	6
carver	1	3	3
chairmaker		3	1
chocolate mak.		1	
coachmaker		4	6
confectioner		1	
cooper	1	10	13
currier		1	1
cutler			1
distiller		5	4
dray maker			1
drayman		4	1
draymaster		1	1
dyer		1	
engraver	1	3	2

	1782	1790	1794
fisherman		3	
gardener		5	
gilder	1	2	1
glazier	1	3	
goldsmith	1	2	
gunsmith		4	5
hackney-coach			1
hair dresser		12	7
harness maker		1	1
hatter		4	3
house carpenter		4	2
jew butcher			1
joiner			2
leatherdresser	1		
limner		2	3
livery stables		1	
lumber measurer		3	1
mahog. sawyer		1	
mantuamaker		3	2
milliner (millener)	2	1	2
miniat. paint.		1	
organ builder			1
painter	1	12	10
printer	4	6	5

	1782	1790	1794
ropemaker		1	1
saddler (sadler)	1	10	10
sail-maker		5	4
seamstress		2	
segar maker		5	1
ship carpenter	1	8	11
ship joiner		2	1
ship wright		8	2
shoemaker	2	23	18
silversmith	5	10	16
starch maker			2
staymaker		1	1
stonecutter		1	1
sugarbaker		1	
tallow-chandler		4	6
tanner		9	10
taylor	5	49	50
tinman	1	6	6
turner	1	2	3
umbrella mak.		1	1
upholsterer	1	1	2
waggon-yard		4	3
watchmaker	2	1	11
watchman		5	1

	1782	1790	1794
wheelwright		2	1
wood measurer		1	2

Craftsmen

1782

Names	*Occupations*	*Addresses*
Askew, James	silversmith	30 Bay
Austin, Robert	taylor	25 Bay
Baird, Robert	tinman	78 Broad street
Binnie, William	baker	76 Church street
Bower, William	watchmaker	28 Broad street
Boyce, Katharine	milliner	79 Broad street
Brown, James	carpenter	27 Tradd street
Bruce, David	printer	85 Church street
Cooke, James	carpenter	3 St. Michael's Alley
Coram, Thomas	engraver	28 Queen street
Courtney, Thomas	taylor	89 Meeting street
Creighton, Joseph	barber	71 Church street
Donaldson, James	carpenter	9 Tradd street
Doughty, Thomas	carpenter	109 Meeting street
Duncan, James	blacksmith	Beresford's Alley
Ewing, John	baker	74 Tradd street
Fell, Thomas	taylor	93 Church street
Fisher, John	cabinetmaker	29 Meeting street
Gottier, Francis	silversmith	98 Broad street
Grant, John	shoemaker	3 Chalmer's Alley
Grant & Kemmel	saddlers	15 Tradd street
Harper, Thomas	jeweller and goldsmith	9 Bay
Harris, Charles	silversmith	24 Meeting street
Hinds, Patrick	shoemaker	10 Beaufain street
Hornby, William	brewer	7 King street
Lockwood, Joshua	watchmaker	1 Broad street
M'Kimmy, Mackie & Cameron	coopers	3 Bedon's Alley
Milling & Oliver	painters & glaziers	93 Meeting street
Mills & Hicks	printers & stationers	12 Broad street
Morgan, Charles	bookbinder & stationer	106 Broad street
Myot, John	silversmith	32 Broad street
Parkinson, John	carver and gilder	Moore street
Patterson, William	carpenter	63 King street
Robertson, James	printer	20 Broad street

Names	Occupations	Addresses
Russell, John & William	ship carpenters	1 Pinckney street
Schume, Conrod	baker	27 Meeting street
Smith, Nicholas	silversmith	29 Bay
Smith, Solomon	upholsterer	8 Tradd street
Snead, James	turner	92 Church street
Stent, Samuel	taylor	22 Church street
Swanson, David	blacksmith	Burn's Wharf
Thomson, Jane	millener	86 Church street
Vinyard, John	leatherdresser	1 Moore street
Warrington, Nicholas	taylor	90 Meeting street
Wells, R. & Sons	printers & booksellers	71 Tradd street
Wright, James	baker	56 Church street

1790

Names	Occupations	Addresses
Abernethie, Thomas	engraver	42 Queen street
Abertie, Francis	segar maker	Waynes court
Adams, William	carpenter	Pinckney street
Aguire, Gugelan	tinman	220 Meeting street
Allison, James	cooper	Beale's wharf
Anthony, John	harness maker	51 Meeting street
Armstrong, William	sadler	90 King street
Arnold, Jonathan	waggon yard	157 King street
Arnold, Matthew	bricklayer	118 King street
Askew, James	watchmaker	96 Broad street
Atkinson, William	carpenter	25 Beresford's alley
Austen, Robert	taylor	51 East bay
Axton, William	lumber meas.	17 King street
Badger, James	painter	93 Queen street
Badger, Jonathan	painter	49 Meeting street
Badger, Joseph	painter	118 Queen street
Barker, Isaac	taylor	11 Eliot street
Barker, William	bricklayer	35 Guinard (*sic*) street
Baylis, William	carpenter	253 Meeting street
Beadon, William	sail maker	Water street
Beard, Robert	tinman	88 Broad street
Beausset, George	barber	5 Tradd street
Bee, Joseph	carpenter	3 Wragg's alley
Beekman, Samuel	blockmaker	50 East bay
Beltzer, Christian	butcher	161 Meeting street
Benbridge, Henry	limner	30 Broad street
Bennea, Peter	ship carpenter	Lynch's lane

Names	*Occupations*	*Addresses*
Bennett, John	carpenter	21 Trott street
Bennett, Thomas	carpenter	74 Church street
Bering, John	silversmith	125 Broad street
Bibean, Francis	carpenter	Union street continued
Bieller, Joseph	butcher	26 Archdale street
Blamyer, William	lumber meas.	Magazine street
Bonneau, Francis	carpenter	58 Broad street
Bowen, Thomas B.	printer	38 East bay
Brown, William	waggon yard	192 King street
Bryan, Samuel	taylor	185 Meeting street
Buckerage, ___	wheelright (*sic*)	Union street continued
Buckmire, Charles	butcher	7 Burns lane
Buckmire, John	butcher	135 King street
Buller, Jacob	butcher	13 Beresford street
Buntin, William	shoemaker	152 Meeting street
Burger, David	gunsmith	31 Queen street
Burn, James	cabinet maker	285 King street
Buro, John	fisherman	3 Ellery street
Burt, William	wood meas.	116 Queen street
Bury, Richard	butcher	14 Beresford street
Butler, Charles P.	silversmith	285 King street
Byrd, Samuel	taylor	39 Union street
Calaghan, John	tallow chand.	40 Tradd street
Cameron, Alexander	dyer	79 Church street
Cameron, David	butcher	15 Trott street
Cane, Conrad	carter	13 Hasell street
Cannon, Daniel	carpenter	22 Queen street
Cantorson, Joshua	limner	104 King street
Carrel, Daniel	silversmith	129 Broad street
Carson, James	printer	136 Tradd street
Castine, John	mahog. sawyer	19 Beresford street
Caveneau, Elizabeth	seamstress	200 King street
Chalmers, Gilbert	carpenter	23 Beaufain street
Chapman, William	sailmaker	27 Archdale street
Charles, James	baker	113 Tradd street
Christie, Alexander	baker	105 Queen street
Chupein, Lewis	hair dresser	37 Church street
Clark, Jeremiah	meas. lumber	Greenwood's wharf
Clark, John	painter	13 Hasell street
Clark, William	sailmaker	36 Pinckney street
Clarke, James	taylor	Jervey's wharf
Clarke, John	watchman	1 Federal green
Clarke and Latham	watchmakers	125 Broad street
Clarkson, Alexander	baker	3 Meeting street
Clements, John	carpenter	49 Queen street
Cobia, Daniel	butcher	18 Beresford street
Cobia, Francis	butcher	161 Meeting street

Names	Occupations	Addresses
Cobia, Nicholas	butcher	36 Archdale street
Collet, William	ship carpenter	114 East bay
Collins, Jonah	hous. carpenter	Wyatt's lot
Colsman, Henry	drayman	Common's street
Cook, Lewis	watchman	14 Beresford's alley
Cook, Thomas	cabinet maker	12 Meeting street
Coram, Thomas	engraver	81 Queen street
Courtney, James	taylor	44 Meeting street
Cox, Susannah	mantuamaker	40 Church street
Crawford & Wallace	paint. & glaz.	18 East bay
Creighton, Joseph	hair dresser	28 Church street
Crook, Shanks	shoemaker	14 Queen street
Cughna, George	shoemaker	76 King street
Darby, William	silversmith	20 Broad street
Davis, Jane	band box mak.	9 Beresfords alley
Dener, George	tanner	3 Mazyck street
Dener, Peter	tanner	5 Dutch church alley
Desel, Charles	cabinet maker	15 Maiden-lane
Desel, Charles	cabinet maker	44 Church street
Devernay, Peter F.	gunsmith	96 Broad street
Dill, Joseph	house carp.	295 King street
Donaldson, James	carpenter	22 Tradd street
Donavan, James	bricklayer	6 Trott street
Dougherty, Patrick	sailmaker	14 Wrag's alley
Dubuard, Peter	hair dresser	235 Meeting street
Duff, John	carter	Barracks
Duncan, Archibald	blacksmith	91 Church street
Duncan, James	blacksmith	18 Beresford's alley
Duncan, Thomas	taylor	117 Queen street
Earnest, Jacob	taylor	276 King street
Eberly, John	baker	17 Guignard street
Eden, Joshua	turner	15 Beresford's alley
Edgeworth, John	drayman	Greenwood's wharf
Elmore, Jesse	taylor	14 Hasell street
Emanuel, Joseph	segar maker	Lynch's lane
Fair, William	shoemaker	5 Elliot street
Felix, Frederick	hair dresser	26 Church street
Ferril, Anthony	segar maker	25½ Elliot street
Finlayson, John	carpenter	4 Trott street
Finlayson, Mungo	cabinet maker	32 Queen street
Fisher, George	butcher	103 Meeting street
Fleming, John	watchman	11 Clifford street
Folker, Gaspar	tanner	11 St. Philip's street
Ford, Batholomew	shoemaker	3 Queen street
Fordham, Richard	ship carpenter	3 Cock lane
Freeman, William	distiller	34 Trott street
Friend, George	baker	39 Union street

Names	*Occupations*	*Addresses*
Friend, Uldy	baker	276 King street
Fuller & Brodie	house carpent.	2 Longitude lane
Gabeau, Anthony	taylor	232 Meeting street
Gardner, William	carver & gilder	206 Meeting street
Geiger, Henry	distiller	Cummins street
Geoghegan, Dominick	sugarbaker	Church street
George, James	ship carpenter	125 East bay
Gerley, John	taylor	4 Mazyck street
Gibbs, George	baker	42 Union street
Gibson, Robert	sadler	242 King street
Given, Robert	stone-cutter	22 Beresford's alley
Glover, William	fisherman	Union street continued
Godfrey, Thomas	carpenter	13 Liberty street
Goodwin, Robert	blacksmith	13 Queen street
Graham, Samuel	blacksmith	3 Longitude lane
Grant, Alexander	baker	148 King street
Grant, John	sadler	88 King Street
Gravenstine, Frederick	taylor	1 Mazyck street
Graves, James	bricklayer	6 Stoll's alley
Gready, James	sadler	85 King street
Greenhill, Hugh & Co.	carpenters	20 Legare street
Gregson, Thomas	brewer	Magazine street
Grenville, James	hair dresser	87 King street
Gressel, George	carpenter	34 Trott street
Gross, Charles	gardener	152 King street
Grott, Francis	gardener	18 Trott street
Gruber, Charles	cooper	80 Queen street
Gruly, Joseph	carpenter	4 Cock lane
Guilleaud, Claudius	baker	8 Elliot street
Gunn, William	blacksmith	6 Queen street
Guy, James	taylor	194 King street
Haig & Dunn	carpenters	116 East bay
Haindsdorff, Henry	carver	15 Hasell street
Hains, Heath	shoemaker	32 Motte's wharf
Hamilton, David	ship carpenter	27 Guignard street
Hamilton, John	carpenter	33 Archdale street
Hampton, William	cabinet maker	13 Beresford's alley
Haney, John	waggon yard	163 King street
Harmond, John	carter	Wentworth street
Harmond, Mitchel	butcher	George street
Harrison, John	shoemaker	25 Broad street
Hart, Dorcas	seamstress	25 Union street continued
Harvey, Benjamin	bricklayer	31 Beaufain street
Hawes, Adoniah	painter	254 King street
Hawkins, James	carpenter	273 King street
Hazlewood, John	painter	36 Pinckney street
Heliger, Joseph	engraver	6 Elliot street

Names	Occupations	Addresses
Henderreckson, Belsha	carpenter	23 Society street
Henri, Peter	miniat. paint.	89 Church street
Henry, Francis	button maker	28 Archdale street
Henry, John	blacksmith	91 Meeting street
Himili, James	watchmaker	126 Broad street
Hinds, Patrick	shoemaker	33 Beaufain street
Hirreld, George	taylor	6 Beresford's alley
Hogarth, William	shoemaker	242 Meeting street
Holbeck, John	bricklayer	8 Moore street
Holland, Hugh	carter	112 East bay
Holmes, Thomas	sadler	264 King street
Holt, William	shoemaker	4 Unity alley
Honeywood, Arthur	blacksmith	1 Moore street
Hook, George	carpenter	12 Chambers alley
Hope, Thomas	cabinet maker	15 Friend street
Hornley, Thomas	distiller	214 King street
Hover, John	taylor	7 King street
Howell, John	hair dresser	223 King street
Hudson, Mary	mantuamaker	34 King street
Hughes, John	ship joiner	Wraggs alley
Hunt, Thomas	brewer	30 Elliot street
Hutchinson, Jeremiah	chair maker	Meeting street
Inglesby, William	taylor	36 Church street
Irons, Berry	taylor	18 Clifford's alley
Irving, James	carpenter	Roper's wharf
Jacks, James	watchmaker	44 East bay
Jackson, John	butcher	12 Liberty street
Jackson, John	watchmaker	129 Broad street
Johnson, John	waggon yard	165 King street
Johnson, William	blacksmith	10 Charles street
Johnston, Jacob	carpenter	2 Boundary street
Johnston, William	hair dresser	49 Church street
Johnston & Wallace	bricklayers	11 Union Street continued
Jolly, Maybury	hatter	111 Queen street
Jones, Jesse	tanner	25 King street
Jones, William	cabinet maker	51 Broad street
Kean, David	coachmaker	29 Archdale street
Kemmell, John	sadler	46 Queen street
Kerr, John	hatter	14 Trott street
Kershaw, John	silversmith	97 Broad street
Know, Conrad	butcher	145 Meeting street
Kosskey, Anthony Jan	blacksmith	23 Beresford alley
Kraps, Andrew	baker	49 King street
Lancaster, William	printer	14 Wragg's alley
Larrey, Robert	carpenter	62 Church street
Latham, Daniel	distiller	2 Hasell street
Lawrence, Estel	shipwright	15 Pinckney street

Names	Occupations	Addresses
Lebbey, Nathaniel	blockmaker	83 East bay
Lee, Stephen	watchmaker	42 Broad street
Lee, William	watchmaker	91 & 95 Broad street
Legge, Samuel	carpenter	38 Archdale street
Lenneau, Bazil	tanner	25 Beaufain street
Levaux, John	carpenter	37 Trott street
Lewie & Coulback	fisherman	3 Union street continued
Liber, John	shoemaker	164 King street
Liblong, Henry	shoemaker	160 King street
Little, Robert	carpenter	9 Wragg's alley
Long, Edward	taylor	3 Queen street
Long, Lewis	carter	179 Meeting street
Luckie, John	sadler	65 King street
Lunt, William	tallow chand.	16 Chalmer's alley
Lynch, James	coachmaker	78 Meeting street
Lyon, Abraham	blacksmith	6 Short street
Lyon, Mordecai	taylor	231 King street
M'Arthur, John	shoemaker	9 Union street continued
M'Call, John	taylor	78 East bay
M'Callister, John	staymaker	246 Meeting street
M'Connell, William	taylor	2 Elliot street
M'Corkel, Samuel	carpenter	132 Queen street
M'Donald, Archibald	taylor	49 Church street
M'Iver, John	printer	23 Tradd street
M'Kenzie, Kennedy	butcher	29 Society street
Mackie, James	cooper	4 Bedon's alley
M'Kimmy, John	bricklayer	28 King street
M'Kimmy, William	cooper	Lynch's lane
M'Lean, Evan	taylor	35 Church street
M'Lean, Lachlan	taylor	40 Church street
M'Nab, Alexander	watchman	35 Meeting street
M'Neil, Archibald	hatter	36 Broad street
Main, Thomas	shipwright	1 Mey's alley
Malland, Charles	carpenter	9 Clifford street
Manson, George	shipwright	3 Ellery street
Mark, Conrad	cooper	276 King street
Markland, John	printer	40 Tradd street
Markland & M'Iver	printers	47 East bay
Marks, Joseph	ship carpenter	8 Pinckney street
Marshall, John	cabinet maker	219 Meeting street
Martin, Chresham	tanner	144 Meeting street
Martin, Daniel	watchmaker	44 King street
Martin, Edward	bricklayer	113 East bay
Matlack, William	watchmaker	20 Broad street
May, George	ship joiner	126 East bay
Mers, John	brassfounder	64 Meeting street
Michael, John	distiller	36 Pinckney street

Names	Occupations	Addresses
Middleton & Ramsey	taylors	43 Queen street
Midford, George	shipwright	6 Chalmers alley
Miller, Benjamin	butcher	8 Burne's lane
Miller, John David	silversmith	109 Broad street
Miller, Nicholas	baker	3 Wentworth street
Miller, Samuel	carpenter	27 Trott street
Milligan and M'Kune	carpenters	85 Church street
Mills, George	shoemaker	77 King street
Mills, William	taylor	105 Church street
Milner, Daniel	chairmaker	272 Meeting street
Milner, George	blacksmith	Cochran's wharf
Milner, John	gunsmith	Snitter's alley
Mintsing, Christian	blacksmith	78 King street
Miott, John	silversmith	230 Meeting street
Mitchell, William	carpenter	32 Guignard street
Moer, William	cooper	Gadsden's wharf
Moncrieff, John	carpenter	102 East bay
Mood, Peter	silversmith	238 King street
Moore, John	butcher	19 Hasell street
Moore, Richard	paint. & glaz.	102 King street
Moore, Thomas	butcher	171 Meeting street
Moore and Denny	sadlers	202 King street
Morgan, Charles	shipwright	36 Trott street
Morris, George	paint. & glaz.	Lynch's lane
Morrison, Ann	milliner	105½ Church street
Muirhead, James	bookbinder	7 Elliot street
Munary, Robert	shoemaker	75 King street
Murphy, John	gardener	3 Boundary street
Murray, Thomas	cooper	91 Church street
Myer, Philip	baker	272 King street
Myers, Samuel	taylor	233 King street
Mylne, James	baker	20 Union street
Neifer, Henry	baker	11 Beresford street
Neifer, Philip	baker	84 King street
Nicholas, Christopher	carter	10 Burne's lane
Nipper, David Henry	bookbinder	225 King street
Oldman, Joseph	confectioner	221 Meeting street
Oliphant, David	painter	66 King street
Palmer, Job	carpenter	26 Trott street
Parker, John & George	brickmakers	80 East bay
Parker, Joseph	butcher	114 East bay
Parkinson, John	carver & gilder	4 Moore street
Parrie, Murraline	baker	20 Beresford's alley
Patterson, William	carpenter	271 King street
Peak, John	taylor	Magazine street
Pelton, Roderick	shoemaker	28 Queen street
Pemble, David	taylor	584 East bay

Names	*Occupations*	*Addresses*
Pencil, Emanuel	tinman	48 Meeting street
Philips, John Christian	baker	105 King street
Philips, Thomas	sadler	62 King street
Philips, Thomas	coachmaker	73 Meeting street
Pierce, Benjamin	painter	35 Broad street
Pierce, Robert	bricklayer	35 Meeting street
Pinger, Lewis	hair dresser	62 East bay
Plumb, Jacob	baker	169 King street
Pope, Alexander	carpenter	94 Queen street
Pope, Samuel	carpenter	4 Pinckney street
Poyas, John Lewis	house carpenter	38 Guignard street
Prentice, John	coachmaker	29 Archdale street
Prince, Charles	tinman	267 King street
Pritchard, Paul	shipwright	88 East bay
Prott, Peter	draymaster	St. Philip's street
Purcell & Hoburne	carpenters	43 Trott street
Purse, William	watchmaker	30 Broad street
Quan, Robert	hair dresser	Queen street
Quin, James	painter	5 Chalmer's alley
Quinby, Henry	carpenter	78 Meeting street
Rader, Philip	shoemaker	118 Broad street
Ralph, John	cabinet maker	52 Church street
Ransier, J. L.	gunsmith	210 King street
Read, John	wheelwright	210 Meeting street
Reader, George	butcher	10 Society street
Rechon, David	taylor	110 King street
Redmond, Andrew	turner	80 Church street
Reeves, Enos	goldsmith	234 Meeting street
Rester, Henry	watchman	119 Meeting street
Reyley, John	blacksmith	9 Ellery street
Reynolds, George	gardener	42 George street
Richards, Gasper	taylor	64 Queen street
Ridfield, Christopher	drayman	Sugar-house yard
Righton, Joseph	cooper	118 Church street
Righton, M'Cully	cooper	120 Church street
Rimeli, Martin	carpenter	Commin's street
Rivers, Francis	carpenter	5 Wragg's alley
Rivers, Samuel	shipwright	4 Water street
Rivers, Thomas	butcher	1 Water street
Roberts, Thomas	carpenter	24 Queen street
Roberts, William	chairmaker	87 Queen street
Robinson, John	bricklayer	5 Cock lane
Robinson, Joseph	carpenter	39½ Meeting street
Rogers, Christopher	taylor	25 Tradd street
Roggaman, Anthony	taylor	85 Church street
Rolinbury, Francis	carpenter	10 Trott street
Roper, Joseph	turner	13 Pinckney street

Names	Occupations	Addresses
Rose, Jeremiah	taylor	40 Church street
Ross, George	tinman	115 Tradd street
Ross, Malcolm	carpenter	29 Society street
Roupel, Daniel	umbrel. maker	226 Meeting street
Rouse, James	currier	87 King street
Rouse, William	shoemaker	3 Tradd street
Rout, Michael	carter	1 Boundary street
Ruberry, John	taylor	115 Queen street
Rumney, Joseph	chocolate mak.	99 East bay
Rush, Matthias	taylor	243 King street
Russell, Benjamin	bricklayer	31 Guignard street
Sailor, David	cooper	38 Elliot street
Sandiford, James	taylor	4 Magazine street
Sass, Jacob	cabinet maker	40 Queen street
Scott, David	bricklayer	Quince's street
Scottow, Samuel	carpenter	181 King street
Seavers, Abraham	carpenter	33 Pinckney street
Secress, Martin	taylor	Lynch's lane
Seixas, Michael	tallow chandler	112 King street
Seller, Michael	tanner	11 Archdale street
Seller, Philip	baker	172 Meeting street
Shaffer, Henry	carter	28 Beaufain street
Shelback, Charles	baker	2 Union street
Shier, John	carpenter	Commin's street
Shrewsbury, Edward	shipwright	132 East bay
Shrewsbury, Stephen	carpenter	12 Guignard street
Shum, Conrad	baker	244 Meeting street
Simpson, Mary	baker	17 Union street continued
Singleton, Daniel	bricklayer	25 Trott street
Siser, Michael	baker	113 King street
Sisley, Lewis	baker	2 Beresford street
Slowman, Henry	taylor	Wyatt's lot
Slowman, John	taylor	36 Tradd street
Smith, John	baker	42 Queen street
Smith, Peter	carpenter	35 Archdale street
Smith, Samuel	carpenter	21 Hasell street
Snitter, Charles	ropemaker	Snitter's alley
Snyder, Paul	carpenter	109 King street
Sommers, John	carpenter	27 Hasell street
Spears, James	carpenter	7 Society street
Spencer, Sebastian	shoemaker	203 Meeting street
Spidle, George	tanner	6 Dutch church alley
Spinler, Jacob	hair dresser	46 East bay
Sproul, Alexander	shoemaker	15 King street
Squibb, Robert	gardener	Savage's Green
Steadman, Charles	carpenter	33 Trott street
Steadman, James	carpenter	110 East bay

Names	Occupations	Addresses
Stent, Samuel	taylor	98 Church street
Stevenson, John	carpenter	88 Queen street
Stoll, Jacob	tinman	189 King street
Stoops, Benjamin	shoemaker	9 Union street
Strobel, Daniel	tanner	149 Meeting street
Strobel, Jacob	butcher	3 Magazine street
Sudor, Elizabeth	segar maker	35 Meeting street
Sudor, Peter	segar maker	28 Union street
Sutton, John	carpenter	178 Meeting street
Switzer, John Rodolph	sadler	23 King street
Symonds, Francis	baker	33 Union street
Tash, Edward	blacksmith	12 Queen street
Taylor, John	silversmith	17 Beresford's alley
Taylor, Paul	carpenter	38 Trott street
Taylor, William	bricklayer	2 Charles street
Tew, Thomas	bricklayer	10 King street
Thomas, John	hair dresser	25 Elliot street
Thomas, Stephen	taylor	34 Elliot street
Thompson, James	taylor	120 Queen street
Thompson, James	carpenter	2 Queen street
Thompson, Peter	carpenter	115 East bay
Thorn, John	sailmaker	21 Guignard street
Threadcraft, Bethel	watchmaker	255 King street
Toole, John	taylor	41 Elliott street
Toole, Michael	taylor	9 Queen street
Toomer, Anthony	bricklayer	7 Legare street
Toussiger, James	carpenter	2 Water street
Tragg, Lawrence	bricklayer	253 Meeting street
Trenas, George	baker	32 Beaufain street
Trezevant, Theodore	taylor	44 Church street
Vardell, Robert	taylor	10 Bedon's alley
Velsing, John	baker	Bull street
Veyong, George	carter	George street
Wagner, Christopher	drayman	5 Trott street
Walker, Robert	carpenter	28 Society street
Wallace, Thomas	cabinet maker	237 Meeting street
Walters, William	hatter	224 King street
Warley, George	bricklayer	20 Beaufain street
Washing, Gasper	butcher	136 King street
Washing, George	butcher	146 Meeting street
Washing, John	butcher	Meeting street
Watson, John	cabinet maker	21 Tradd street
Watson, John & George	upholsterers	104 Church street
Watts, Charles	cabinet maker	237 Meeting street
Watts, John	carpenter	Wyatt's lot
Wayne, Sarah	mantuamaker	16 Beresford's alley
Weare, Peter	shoemaker	15 Clifford street

Names	Occupations	Addresses
Welch, George	baker	21 Trott street
Westermyer, Henry	goldsmith	23 Church street
Whieldon, Joseph	taylor	7 Elliot street
Wightman, William	silversmith	236 Meeting street
Wilcocks, John	blacksmith	9 Trott street
Wilkins, James	carpenter	2 Gibbes street
Wilkinson, Richard	livery stables	73 Meeting street
Williams, Mort. John	ship carpenter	6 Charles street
Williamson, John	blacksmith	48 King street
Williman, Christopher	butcher	227 King street
Williman, Jacob	butcher	Harleston's green
Wilson, John	cabinet maker	217 Meeting street
Wilson and M'Kennan	taylors	105½ Church street
Wish, Benjamin	carpenter	12 Mazyck street
Wisinger, John	baker	182 King street
Woodcock, Richard	tallow chandler	241 Meeting street
Woolf, Matthias	butcher	2 Mazyck street
Wright, James	baker	42 Tradd street
Wyatt, Peter	carpenter	Wyatt's lot
Yates, Seth	ship carpenter	Wayne's court
Young, George	butcher	25 Guignard street
Young, John	hair dresser	East bay
Zealy, James	shoemaker	298 King street

1794

Names	Occupations	Addresses
Abernethie, Thomas	engraver	42 Queen street
Adams, William	ship joiner	90 East bay
Aiguire, Gayton	tinman	221 Meeting street
Allen, Thomas	ship carpenter	5 Charles street
Allison, James	cooper	5 Elliott continued
Anderson, ___	stay maker	Elliott street
Anthony, John	harness maker	51 Meeting street
Appelton, John	carpenter	25 Meeting street
Armstrong, William	saddler	75 King street
Atmar, Ralph, jun.	silversmith	49 Meeting street
Atwell, Ichabod	wood measurer	62 Church street
Austin, Robert	taylor	50 East bay
Axson, William, jun.	carpenter	127 Church street
Axson, William, sen.	lumber measu.	17 King street
Badger, James	painter	56 King street
Badger, John	painter	38 Broad street

Names	*Occupations*	*Addresses*
Badger, Joseph	painter	17 Pinckney street
Baker, Francis	bricklayer	33 King street
Bals, Thomas	blockmaker	8 Bedons alley
Balton, Andrew	barber	137 Queen street
Barker, Joseph	carpenter	12 Hasell street
Barr, Jacob	waggon yard	219 King street
Baylis, William	carpenter	253 Meeting street
Beard, Robert	tinman	88 Broad street
Bedon, George	carpenter	8 Hopton's lane
Beedom, William	sail maker	7 Water street
Beekman, Samuel	blockmaker	112 Queen street
Belser, Christian	butcher	151 Meeting street
Bennett, Asher	carpenter	58 Queen street
Bennett, John	carpenter	Bennett's mills
Bennett, Thomas	carpenter	Harlestons green
Bennica, Peter	ship carpenter	Lynch's lane
Bering, John	silversmith	125 Broad street
Bevin, Francis	carpenter	11 Union continued
Bird, Reading	butcher	103½ Meeting street
Boiler, Joseph	butcher	26 Archdale street
Bonfall, Samuel	blacksmith	5 Wentworth street
Bonneau, Francis	house carpenter	58 Broad street
Boothe, Thomas	carpenter	7 Stoll's alley
Boswell, James	painter	11 Clifford's alley
Bowen & Elliott	painters	9 Queen street
Bowen & Harrison	printers	38 East bay
Bradford, Thomas	cabinet maker	30 Broad street
Brally, Thomas	waggon yard	221 King street
Brodie, Robert	carpenter	16 Lynch's lane
Brown, Squire ___	barber	20 Tradd street
Buckham, Jacob	gunsmith	9 Queen street
Buffet, George	barber	5 Tradd street
Burger, David	gunsmith	21 Queen street
Burkmeyer, Charles	butcher	7 Burn's lane
Burkmeyer, John	butcher	Pitt street
Burns, James	cabinet maker	234 King street
Butler, Charles P.	silversmith	255 King street
Cain, Conrad	carter	34½ Trott street
Callaghan, John	tallow-chandler	39 Tradd street
Camnon, David	butcher	Trott street
Cannon, Daniel	carpenter	22 Queen street
Canter, Joshua	limner	260 King street
Carrell, Daniel	silversmith	124 Broad street
Cart, Joseph	silversmith	33 Guignard street
Casey, Benjamin	coachmaker	46 Meeting street
Casey, Benjamin	coachmaker	47 Meeting street
Caveneau, James	carter	Pinckney street
Chambers, Gilbert	carpenter	23 Beaufain street

Names	Occupations	Addresses
Charles, Henry	carpenter	Wyatt's lot
Charles, James	baker	113 Tradd street
Chrietzburgh, Michael	taylor	Hopton's lane
Christie, Alexander	baker	106 Queen street
Chupein, Lewis	hair dresser	37 Church street
Clarke, Benjamin	cutler	33 Beaufain street
Clarke, David	watchmaker	5 Price's alley
Clarke, James	taylor	11 Elliott street
Clarke, John	butcher	22 Trott street
Clarke, William	sailmaker	7 Pinckney street
Clastier, Maxemellian	starch-maker	15 Berresford street
Clement, John	carpenter	47 Queen street
Cole, Thomas	bricklayer	2 Trott street
Conner, Bryan	butcher	156 King street
Cook, Thomas	carpenter	12 Meeting street
Coram, Thomas	engraver	81 Queen street
Courtney, James	taylor	44 Meeting street
Cowin, John	hatter	16 Chambers' alley
Cox, Susannah	mantuamaker	Federal
Crawford, Alexander	painter	258 Meeting street
Creighton, Samuel	barber	Amen street
Crookshanks, Daniel	shoemaker	2 Broad street
Crookshanks, Daniel	shoemaker	17 Clifford's alley
Crookshanks, William	starch-maker	Bull street
Curtis, ___	saddler	Society street
Day, George	silversmith	10 Trott street
Debow, John	silversmith	118 Queen street
Delorme, Francis	upholsterer	115 Tradd street
Dener, George	tanner	Magazine street
Dener, Peter	currier	5 Allen street
Denny, Samuel	saddler	111 King street
Desell, Charles	cabinet-maker	51 Broad street
Desverneys, Anthony P.	gunsmith	97 Broad street
Dickenson, Joseph	carpenter	40 King street
Dill, Joseph, senior	carpenter	295 King street
Dodge, Joseph	ship carpenter	1 Lodge alley
Donaldson, James	carpenter	116 Tradd street
Dougharty, Patrick	sail-maker	13 Amen street
Drummond, John	shoemaker	40 Elliott street
Dubnard, Peter	barber	99 Tradd street
Duncan, ___	baker	42½ Queen street
Duncan, James	blacksmith	18 Berresford street
Duncan & Murdock	blacksmiths	Church street
Dunn, Alexander	carpenter	Federal
Dupre, Benjamin	taylor	90 Church street
Ebberly, John	baker	17 Guignard street
Echlar, Christopher	taylor	50 King street

Names	*Occupations*	*Addresses*
Edean, Joshua	turner	15 Berresford street
Elfe, Thomas	cabinetmaker	116 Queen street
Ellis, Thomas	woodmeasurer	Scarborough street
Elmore, Jeffy	taylor	35 Church street
Eyers, Thomas	taylor	7 Maiden-lane
Fair, William	shoemaker	26 Broad street
Fair, William	tanner	Montague street
Fairchild, Aaron	blacksmith	17 Pinckney street
Fell, Elizabeth	milliner	23 Broad street
Fife, James	cooper	Whim's court
Finlayson, Mrs. ___	cabinet-maker	32 Queen street
Folker, John Casper	shoemaker	11 St. Philip's
Fordham, Richard	ship carpenter	Cock lane
Fowler, Richard	carpenter	Wyatt's lot
Fowler & Brodie	carpenters	5 Longitude lane
Friend, Ulrick	baker	½ Trott street
Frist, John	carter	44 King street
Fry, Thomas	taylor	98 Tradd street
Gabeau, Anthony	taylor	232 Meeting street
Gardner, William	carver & gilder	47 Broad street
George, James	shipwright	up the path 3 miles
Gerley, John	taylor	Mazyck street
Gesken, Henry	cabinet-maker	205 King street
Gibbs, George	baker	28 Elliott street
Gibson, Robert	saddler	249 King street
Gitsenger, George	shoemaker	77 King street
Given, Robert	stone-cutter	Federal
Godfrey, Thomas	house carpenter	14 Allen street
Gordon, Andrew	bricklayer	13 Moore street
Gordon, James	bricklayer	11 Moore street
Gordon, James	shoemaker	
Gourlay, John	shoemaker	185 Meeting street
Gourlay, John	shoemaker	50 Meeting street
Graham, Samuel	blacksmith	6 Longitude lane
Grainger, James	chair-maker	15 Guignard street
Grant, Alexander	baker	148 King street
Granville, James	hair dresser	85 King street
Grassell, George	carpenter	Quince street
Gravanstine, Frederick	taylor	2 Mazyck street
Greerly, Joseph	carpenter	Cock lane
Gruber, Charles, senior	cooper	79 Queen street
Gruber, Samuel	cooper	St. Philip's street
Guillaud, Claudius	baker	9 Elliott street
Gunn, William	gunsmith	6 Queen street
Guy, James	taylor	193 Meeting street
Hadden, Gardner	taylor	85 Church street
Haig, David	cooper	112 East bay

Names	*Occupations*	*Addresses*
Haig & Dunn	carpenters	101 Meeting street
Haig & Murray	coopers	90 Church street
Hainsdorf, Henry	carver	14 Hasell street
Hambord, Godfrey	carpenter	13 Lynch's lane
Hamilton, David	shipwright	27 Guignard street
Hamlin & Clessey	saddlers	32 Church street
Harley, William	butcher	Society street
Harman, John	carter	Cumming street
Harvey, Benjamin	bricklayer	35 Beaufain street
Hawkins, James	cabinet-maker	94 Tradd street
Hazelwood, ___	painter	15 Queen street
Henrichsen, Betye	carpenter	Society street
Henry, George	shoemaker	1 Elliott street
Heyneman, Valentine	watchman	20 George street
Hill, Jonathan	baker	
Hill, Paul	distiller	1 Berresford street
Himelie, John James	watchmaker	119 Broad street
Hinds, Patrick	shoemaker	37 Beaufain street
Hobart, John	taylor	1 Berresford street
Hogsden, Mary	mantau-maker (*sic*)	36 King street
Holmes, Thomas	saddler	28 Archdale street
Honeywood, Elizabeth	blacksmith	1 Moore street
Horlbeck, John	bricklayer	8 Moore street
Hornby, Thomas	distiller	214 King street
Howard, John	hair dresser	225 King street
Huck, Michael	hackney-coach	264 King street
Hughes, John	carpenter	2 Wragg's alley
Hunter, William	taylor	2 Elliott street
Hurst, Charles	taylor	49 Church street
Inglesby, Henry	taylor	23 Tradd street
Inglesby, William	taylor	24 Tradd street
Jeffords, John	taylor	18 Pinckney street
Jenny, John	baker	2 Berresford street
Johnson, Isaac	taylor	14 Friend street
Johnson, W. I.	watchmaker	93 King street
Johnson, William	blacksmith	7 Charles street
Johnston, Robert	taylor	128 Broad street
Jones, Henry	carpenter	3 Lodge alley
Kay, James	bricklayer	291 King street
Kay, Joseph	butcher	9 Trott street
Kerr, John	hatter	111 Queen street
Kershaw, Joseph	silversmith	6 Market square
King, Charles	taylor	91 King street
Kingman, Eliab	hair dresser	4 Elliott street
Knoff, Conrad	butcher	146 Meeting street
Lampe, John	watchmaker	118 Tradd street
Lane, Samuel	carpenter	Maiden lane

Names	*Occupations*	*Addresses*
Lanneau, Brazill	tanner	Pitt street
Larabert, Frederick	tallow-chandler	Cumming street
Larry, Robert	carpenter	62 Church street
Latham, Daniel	distiller	2 Hasell street
Leblanc, Henry	shoemaker	115 King street
Lee, William	watchmaker	91 Broad street
Levoux, John	carpenter	37 Trott street
Lewis, Henry	taylor	300 King street
Libby, Nathaniel	blockmaker	7 Wragg's alley
Little, Robert	carpenter	12 Amen street
Luckie, John	saddler	246 King street
Lunt, Mary	tallow-chandler	13 Union street
M'Call, John	taylor	78 East bay
M'Clish, Alexander	brass founder	64 Meeting street
M'Iver, John	printer	111 Tradd street
M'Kenny, George	taylor	3 Elliott street
Mackey, Crafts	watchmaker	61 East bay
Mackie & Williams	coachmaker	1 Federal street
M'Kimmy, John	bricklayer	28 King street
M'Lean, Evan	taylor	230 Meeting street
M'Mullen, Richard	waggon-yard	158 King street
Maden & Woodworth	hatters	12 Elliott street
Magan, Patrick	watchmaker	45 East bay
Makkay, John	carpenter	33 Trott street
Manning, Hugh	carpenter	9 Amen street
Markland, John	printer	5 Union continued
Markland, M'Iver & Co.	printers	47 East bay
Marshall, John	cabinet-maker	219 Meeting street
Martin, Christian	tanner	145 Meeting street
Martin, Jacob	tanner	214 Meeting street
Mattuce, John	butcher	13 Magazine street
Merrell, Benjamin	taylor	45 Church street
Meyer, Philip	baker	42 Union street
Michael, John	distiller	29 Pinckney street
Middleton & Ramsay	taylors	19 Elliott street
Miller, John	carpenter	288 King street
Miller, John David	silversmith	109 Broad street
Miller, John James	carpenter	73 Meeting street
Miller, Nicholas	baker	4 Wentworth street
Miller, William	taylor	58½ East bay
Milligan, Joseph	tallow-chandler	72 King street
Mills, William	taylor	105 Church street
Milner, Daniel	coachmaker	251 Meeting street
Milner, George	blacksmith	26 Guignard street
Minizing, Philip	blacksmith	78 King street
Miott, John	silversmith	39 Trott street
Mitchell, Florine	painter	27 Hasell street

Names	Occupations	Addresses
Mood, Peter	silversmith	238 King street
Moore, John	butcher	58 George street
Moore, Joseph	draymaster	100 East bay
Moore, Philip	cabinet-maker	246 Meeting street
Morgan, Charles	ship carpenter	1 Pinckney street
Mortimore, John	carpenter	3 Moore street
Morton, William	butcher	102 Meeting street
Muirhead, James	bookbinder	7 Elliott street
Muncrieff, John	carpenter	102 East bay
Munro, John	watchmaker	Elliott street
Murray, Thomas	cooper	91 Church street
Muzier, Francis	barber	1 Champney's row
Myers, ___	baker	Union street
Myers, Israel	jew butcher	15 Union continued
Myers, Samuel	taylor	232½ King street
Mylne, James	baker	20 Union street
Naser, Mrs. Henry	baker	11 Berresford street
Naser, Philip	baker	34 King street
Nelson, ___	silversmith	21 Trott street
Nelson, Andrew	baker	90 King street
Nelson, Francis	ship carpenter	116 East bay
Nevil, Joshua	cabinet-maker	6 Clifford's alley
Nicks, William	butcher	24 Trott street
Nipper, David	bookbinder	99 King street
Nobbs, Samuel	barber	56 King street
Norris, George	saddler	90 King street
Norris, James	painter	26 Queen street
Notherman, Harmon	blacksmith	187 King street
Odin, Anthony	limner	2 Market square
O'Donnald, James	cooper	Pinckney street
Oliphant, David	limner	8 South bay
Palmer, John	carpenter	26 Trott street
Parker, George	brickmaker	Scarborough street
Parker, John	brickmaker	Scarborough street
Parker, John	butcher	115 East bay
Parkinson, John	carver	5 Moore street
Parks, John	shoemaker	26 Union street
Patterson, William	carpenter	271 King street
Pearse, John	painter	8 Elliott street
Peebles, James	carpenter	41 Trott street
Peignea, Lewis	hair dresser	62 East bay
Pellason, Guilliam	tallow-chandler	21 Berresford street
Pencill, Emanuel	tinman	47 Meeting street
Philips, John C.	baker	105 King street
Piott, Peter	draymaker	9 St. Philip's street
Plumb, Jacob	baker	147 King street
Poyas, Daniel	carpenter	Wyatt's lot

Names	*Occupations*	*Addresses*
Poyas, John Lewis	carpenter	6 Guignard street
Prentice, John	coachmaker	Archdale street
Price, Sarah	milliner	34 Broad street
Prince, Charles	tinman	265 King street
Pritchard, William	ship carpenter	2 Charles street
Purce, William	watchmaker	236 Meeting street
Quinby, Henry	carpenter	Quince street
Quinby, Joseph	carpenter	5 Pinckney street
Ralph & Silberg	cabinet-maker	52 Church street
Ransier, Lambert	gunsmith	210 King street
Read & King	tinman	90 Church street
Reeves, Enos	silversmith	234 Meeting street
Reid, John	wheelwright	213 Meeting street
Reid, Walter	blacksmith	48 King street
Reyley, John	blacksmith	77 Meeting street
Reynolds, George	carpenter	42 George street
Richards, Gasper	taylor	16 Clifford's alley
Richardson, Barney	carpenter	Wyatt's square
Richon, David	taylor	110 King street
Righton, Joseph	cooper	10 Stoll's alley
Righton, M'Cully	cooper	120 Church street
Rivers, Beulah	cake-maker	St. Michael's alley
Rivers, James	carpenter	53 Church street
Rivers, Samuel	carpenter	4 Water street
Rivers, Thomas	butcher	40 Trott street
Robb, Michael	shoemaker	6 Elliott street
Roberts, John	taylor	34 Church street
Roberts, William	coach-maker	88 Queen street
Robinett, Francis	cooper	1 Unity alley
Robinson, John	bricklayer	Cock lane
Robinson, Joseph	carpenter	277 King street
Rogers, Christopher	taylor	25 Tradd street
Roper, Joseph	turner	13 Pinckney street
Rosanbohm, Francis	carpenter	11 Trott street
Roston, Lewis	watchmaker	133 King street
Roupell, Daniel	umbrella-mak.	226 Meeting street
Rouse, William	tanner	75 Meeting street
Rousseau, Peter	taylor	133 Queen street
Rowe, Michael	carter	21 George street
Ruberry, John	taylor	115 Queen street
Rush, Mathias	taylor	243 King street
Russell, Benjamin	bricklayer	31 Guignard street
Russell, George	ship carpenter	19 Lynch's lane
Russell, John	turner	85 Meeting street
Sansellery, Peter	barber	24 Elliott street
Sass, Jacob	cabinet-maker	40 Queen street
Sawyer, George	shoemaker	14 Berresford street

Names	Occupations	Addresses
Schultz, Daniel	carpenter	27½ Hasell street
Seavers, Abraham	carpenter	35 Pinckney street
Sellar, Michael	tanner	Archdale street
Shaffer, Henry	carter	32 Beaufain street
Shallier, Martin	taylor	19 Berresford street
Shaw & Ewing	carpenter	59 King street
Sherry, Arthur	cooper	13 Bedon's alley
Shirer, John	carpenter	Cumming street
Shrewsberry, Stephen	carpenter	33 Archdale street
Simmons, William	taylor	224 King street
Smith, Peter	carpenter	35 Archdale street
Smith, Samuel	carpenter	174 Meeting street
Smith, William	taylor	240 King street
Snitter, Charles	rope-maker	2 Rope lane, M.
Spears, James	carpenter	6 Society street
Spiessager, John	organ builder	6 Legare street
Spinler, Joseph	hair dresser	46 East bay
Stacker, Christopher	butcher	4 Allen street
Steadman, James	carpenter	167 Meeting street
Stent, Samuel	taylor	42 Church street
Stevenson, John	carpenter	89 Queen street
Stewart, John	tallow-chandler	21 Union street
Stoll, Jacob	tinman	129 King street
Stone & Purcell	saddlers	82 King street
Stoops, Benjamin T.	shoemaker	103 Meeting street
Stroble, Daniel	tanner	148 Meeting street
Stroble, Jacob	butcher	Magazine street
Suder, Peter, junior	segar-maker	28 Union street
Sutton, Richard	cooper	19 Union continued
Switzer, John Rodolph	saddler	234 King street
Tash, Edward	blacksmith	12 Queen street
Taylor, Paul	carpenter	38 Trott street
Tew, John	taylor	41 Elliott street
Tew, Thomas	bricklayer	10 King street
Thomas, John	barber	25 Elliott street
Thomas, Stephen	taylor	32 Elliott street
Thorn, John G.	sailmaker	23 Guignard street
Threadcraft, Bethel	watchmaker	254 King street
Timothy, Benjamin F.	printer	84 Broad street
Tool, Michael	taylor	34 Union street
Toomer, Anthony	bricklayer	7 Legare street
Trezevant, Theodore	taylor	43 Church street
Vacanna, ___	joiner	Trott street
Vardell, Robert	taylor	10 Bedon's alley
Vliex, Frederick	barber	25 Church street
Wagner, Christopher	drayman	6 Trott street
Wallis, Hugh	painter	33 Tradd street

Names	*Occupations*	*Addresses*
Wallis, Thomas	cabinet-maker	231 Meeting street
Wallis, William	cabinet-maker	175 Meeting street
Warson, Thomas	carpenter	5 Stoll's alley
Watson, John	upholsterer	104 Church street
Watson, Joseph	hair dresser	98 Broad street
Watts, Charles	cabinet-maker	5 Market square
Weaver, Peter	shoemaker	151 King street
Welch, Thomas	baker	2 Union street
Wershing, John	butcher	8 Burns' lane
Wessinger, John	baker	181 King street
Westermyer, Andrew	silversmith	23 Church street
White, Blake Leay	carpenter	41 King street
Whiteman, William	silversmith	226 Meeting street
Whittimore, Retun	joiner	44 Church street
Wileseks, Jeremiah	painter	5 Berresford's alley
Wilkins, James	carpenter	Wentworth street
Willeman, Christopher	tanner	227 King street
Williams, Isham	ship carpenter	103 East bay
Williams, John M.	ship carpenter	4 Charles street
Williams, Joseph	taylor	Hasell street
Williman, Jacob	tanner	Montague street
Wilson, John	cabinet-maker	95 Meeting street
Wilson & M'Kinnon	taylors	105½ Church street
Wish, Benjamin	carpenter	61 Queen street
Wittick, Charles	silversmith	237 Meeting street
Woolf, Matthias	butcher	Mazyck street
Wright, James	baker	42 Tradd street
Wyatt, John	carpenter	Wyatts' square
Wyatt, Richard	carpenter	6 Amen street
Yates, Seth	ship carpenter	21 Lynch's lane
Yoer, G. & S.	shoemakers	97 Queen street
Young, George	butcher	5 Guignard street
Young, William Price	printer, bookseller & stationer	43 Broad street

Chapter II / Mercantile Community

Charleston became a major shipping center during the eighteenth century. Its prosperity depended on the export of agricultural products which were grown in the nearby areas. A large portion of the mercantile community of the late eighteenth century depended on the exporting of local products in exchange for products from overseas.

A count of the members of the mercantile community is shown below.

Mercantile Community

	1782	1790	1794
bookseller	1		1
bottle seller		1	1
broker	1	6	10
factor	9	56	48
fruitshop			1
fruitstand		1	
grocer	10	16	26
horsedealer		1	1
indigo broker		1	1
indigo factor			2
insurance broker	2		2
ironmonger		1	1
jeweller	1		1
merchant	98	164	167
music store			1

musick shop		1	
perfumer		1	1
retailer lumber			1
ship chandlers	3	2	1
shop keeper		208	185
stationer	3	1	1
stock jobber			1
store keeper		27	16
tobacconist		1	4
undertaker	1		
vintner		1	2
wharfinger		4	
wine merchant	3	2	1

Mercantile Community

1782

Names	*Occupations*	*Addresses*
Alexander, William	merchant	51 Bay
Ancrum, William & George	merchants	1 Ellery street
Arwin & Rugge	merchants	90 Broad street
Atkins & Weston	merchants	6 Legare street
Atkinson, Joseph	merchant	30 Broad street
Austin, Adam	merchant	41 Broad street
Bentham & Sutcliffe	merchants	104 Broad street
Benthune, John	merchant	10 Elliot street
Blair, James, & Co.	merchants	27 Bay
Blakely, David	grocer	25 Broad street
Brown, Clarkson, & Co.	merchants	28 Broad street
Bryden & Allen	merchants	1 Tradd street
Buchanans & Robb	merchants	4 Bay
Buckle & Trescot	ship chandlers	35 Bay

Names	Occupations	Addresses
Burt, William	factor	11 Gibbes street
Caldwell, Henry	grocer	80 Tradd street
Cam, William	merchant	21 Broad street
Cape, Brian	merchant	84 Church street
Carne, Samuel	merchant	9 Orange street
Carson, William & James	merchants	3 Tradd street
Chambers, John	merchant	23 Bay
Chisolm, Alexander	factor	56 Church street
Cohen, Gershon	merchant	29 Bay
Collins & Hayes	merchants	12 Broad street
Cooke, Jonathan	grocer	24 Bay
Corbett, Edward	merchant	8 Tradd street
Crook & Beard	merchants	91 Church street
Cruden, John	merchant	10 Bay continued
Dart, Benjamin	factor	15 Tradd street
Davie, William	grocer	59 Tradd street
Dow, Alexander	ship chandler	38 Bay
Drysdale, Alexander	merchant	80 Church street
Duncan, George	wine merchant	9 Elliott street
Dupont, Gideon	merchant	77 King street
Edwards, James	factor	76 Tradd street
Fardo, George	factor	110 Meeting street
Farquhar, Robert & Co.	merchants	Tradd street
Foster, Thomas & Seth	merchants	99 Broad street
Gaillard, Theodore	merchant	9 Bay
Geyer, John	merchant	87 Church street
Gickie, William	ship chandler	Bay
Glen, William & Co.	merchants	8 Elliott street
Gordon, James	merchant	90 King street
Granger, Thomas	merchant	81 Tradd street
Grant, John	wine merchant	31 Bay
Gratton, Daniel	merchant	24 Broad street
Greenwood & Legge	merchants	44 Bay
Gregorie, Douglas & Co.	merchants	26 Church street
Harper, Thomas	jeweller and goldsmith	9 Bay
Harris & Blachford	merchants	36 Bay
Inglis, Alexander	merchant	31 Queen street
Inglis, Thomas	merchant	61 Meeting street
Johnston, Charles	merchant	White-Point
Jones, Joseph	grocer	5 Tradd street
Kershaw, William	factor	Greenwood's Wharf
Kingsley & Taylor	merchants	16 Broad street
La Motte, James	merchant	92 Broad street
Lawson & Price	merchants	Bay
Lechmere, Anthony	merchant	7 Bedon's Alley
Legare, Samuel	insurance broker	26 Church street
Lightwood, Edward	merchant	46 Meeting street

Names	*Occupations*	*Addresses*
Lindsay, Robert & William	merchants	46 Bay
Lorimer, Alexander	merchant	15 Broad street
Macbeth, Alexander	merchant	6 Elliott street
M'Call, John	insurance broker	77 Church street
M'Callum & Ewing	merchants	28 Church street
M'Douall, James	merchants	109 Broad street
MacIver, John & Alexander	merchants	100 Broad street
Mackenzie, Andrew & Co.	merchants	41 Bay
M'Lauchlan, Colin	merchant	38 Bay
M'Lellan & Wallace	merchants	40 Bay
M'Murray, James & Co.	merchants	54 Queen street
M'Nair & Maxwell	grocers	Tradd street
M'Whann, William	merchant	Tradd street
Mansell & Corbett	merchants	8 Cumberland street
Manson, John	merchant	4 Bay
Mayott, John	merchant	38 Bay
Michie, Charles	wine merchant	27 Church street
Mills & Hicks	printers and stationers	12 Broad street
Morgan, Charles	bookbinder and stationer	106 Broad street
Mowatt, George & Co.	merchants	71 Church street
Munro, George	grocer	27 Bay
Neufville, Edward	merchant	Bay
Newcomen & Collet	merchants	8 Bedon's alley
Nicholson, John	grocer	45 Bay
Ogilvie, Charles	merchant	10 Bay continued
O'Hara, Daniel	grocer	109 Broad street
O'Hear, James	factor	4 Cumberland street
Oliphant, Alexander	factor	Greenwood's Wharf
Parker & Co.	merchants	6 Bedon's alley
Patton, Robert	merchant	4 Bay
Pearce, Abraham	undertaker	32 Broad street
Penman, James & Edward	merchants	15 Bay
Powell, Hopton & Co.	merchants	5 Bedon's alley
Primrose, Nicol	merchant	3 Broad street
Prout, Robert & William	merchants	89 .Church street
Richardson, John	merchant	6 Broad street
Richardson, John, jun.	merchant	22 Broad street
Rose, Alexander	merchant	37 Tradd street
Ross, William-Kerr	merchant	2 Tradd street
Rowand, Robert	merchant	2 Friend street
Rutherford & Ainslie	merchants	6 Elliott street
Scarbrough & Cooke	merchants	6 Broad street
Shirras, Alexander	grocer	38 Bay
Shoolbred & Moodie	merchants	83 Tradd street
Simons, Maurice	merchant	87 Broad street
Simpson, John & Thomas	merchants	32 Bay
Simpson, Jonathan & William	merchants	27 Church street

Names	Occupations	Addresses
Smith, John	merchant	13 Broad street
Smith, John, jun.	factor	Burn's Wharf
Smith, Julius	merchant	79 Church street
Smith, Roger	merchant	21 Broad street
Smith, William	merchants	33 Bay
Smyth, John	merchant	Ellery street
Snodgrass, William	merchant	94 Church street
Somersall, William	merchant	53 Bay
Somervill & Duguid	merchants	101 Broad street
Stott, Robert	merchant	44 Bay
Teasdale, John	merchant	82 Tradd street
Thompson, John & William	merchants	Tradd street
Thomson, George, jun.	merchant	Greenwood's Wharf
Tufts & Ryan	merchants	26 Bay
Tunno, John & Adam	merchants	48 Bay
Valk, Jacob	broker	109 King street
Wagner, John	merchant	75 Broad
Walker & Maitland	merchants	92 Broad
Warrington, James	merchant	90 Meeting street
Warwick, Anthony & Co.	merchants	90 Church street
Wayne, Richard	merchants	81 Tradd street
Wells, R. & Son	printers and book-sellers	71 Tradd street
White, Gideon	merchant	27 Church street

1790

Names	Occupations	Addresses
Abendanon, Joseph	broker	40 King street
Abrahams, Jacob	shopkeeper	70 East bay
Adams and English	shopkeepers	21 East bay
Alexander, David	merchant	3 Bedon's alley
Alexander, Hector	shopkeeper	Motte's wharf
Alexander, Judah	shopkeeper	10 Clifford street
Allen and Ewing	merchants	120 Tradd street
Anderson, Alexander	grocer	53½ Bay
Anderson, Robert	shopkeeper	240 King street
Armstrong, Fleetwood	shopkeeper	128 East bay
Avon, Solomon	shopkeeper	46 King street
Ball, Thomas	factor	Lynch's lane
Ball and Minott	factor	Vanderhorst's wharf
Baron, John	merchant	120 Broad street
Bartlett, Isaac	merchant	8 Stoll's alley

Names	*Occupations*	*Addresses*
Baruck, Solomon	shopkeeper	246 King street
Beard, Charles	merchant	22 Elliot street
Beatty, Robert	storekeeper	28 Broad street
Bell, John	shopkeeper	150 King street
Bell, William	shopkeeper	248 King street
Below, Joakim	shopkeeper	119 King street
Benjamin, Samuel	shopkeeper	195 King street
Berney, John	merchant	24 East bay
Bethune, Angus	merchant	22 Broad & Church streets
Bethune, Hugh	merchant	269 King street
Biverly, Frederick	shopkeeper	23 Union street continued
Black, John	merchant	12 Broad street
Black, Nathaniel	shopkeeper	7 Ellery street
Blackaller, Oliver	shopkeeper	10 Union street continued
Blacklock, William	merchant	8 Meeting street
Blair, John	shopkeeper	25 Church street
Blake, Edward	factor	1 Legare street
Blake, John	shopkeeper	20 East bay
Blake, John	merchant	29 Elliott street
Blake, John	merchant	213 King street
Blakely, Samuel	storekeeper	28½ Broad street
Bold, Rhodes & Co.	merchants	132 Tradd street
Booner, Christian	shopkeeper	11 Queen street
Bourdeaux, Daniel	merchant	22 Beaufain street
Bradford, William	merchant	43 Meeting street
Braly, Thomas	shopkeeper	220 King street
Brodie, Thomas	factor	105½ Church street
Brown & Hutchinson	shopkeepers	124 Church street
Brownlee, John	merchant	212 King street
Bryan, Arthur	merchant	State House square
Buckle, Thomas	merchant	56 Broad street
Burns, John	shopkeeper	5 Union street
Burrill and Storum	shopkeepers	106 Church street
Bury, Susannah	shopkeeper	197 King street
Buyck, Peter	bottle seller	27 Elliot street
Buyer, John Goodly	shopkeeper	177 Meeting street
Caldwell, Henry	storekeeper	123 Tradd street
Caldwell, Joseph	shopkeeper	215 Meeting street
Calwell, Henry	shopkeeper	24 Church street
Cam, William	merchant	127 Queen street
Cameron, Alexander	shopkeeper	81 King street
Cameron, Lewis	storekeeper	137 Tradd street
Cantor, Jacob	merchant	216 Meeting street
Canty and Solomons	shopkeeper	135 Queen street
Cape, Bryan	factor	91 East bay
Carner, Lawrence	shopkeeper	41 Elliott street
Carpenter, James	shopkeeper	133 Queen street

Names	Occupations	Addresses
Carr, Wilder & Co.	storekeeper	39 Tradd street
Carter, John	shopkeeper	98 Tradd street
Cartmell, William	storekeeper	53 East bay
Cavaneau, James	factor	8 Union street continued
Cazeneau, Edward	merchant	134 Tradd street
Champney, John	wharfinger	94 King street
Cheves, Alexander	shopkeeper	96 King street
Chion, P. G. and Son	merchants	39 East bay
Chisholm, Alex., jun.	factor	18 South bay
Christie, Edward	shopkeeper	93 Church street
Clark, Sarah	shopkeeper	Roper's wharf
Clarke, Mary	shopkeeper	170 King street
Cochran, Bridget	shopkeeper	89 King street
Cochran, Thomas	factor	138 East bay
Coghlan, William	shopkeeper	8 Union street
Cohen, Gershom	factor	140 East bay
Cohen, Gershom	merchant	22 Church street
Cohen, Jacob	shopkeeper	92 King street
Cole, Richard	factorr (*sic*)	213 Meeting street
Condy and Bryan	merchants	4 Champney's row
Connor, Bryan	shopkeeper	Motte's wharf
Connor, Thomas	shopkeeper	Greenwood's wharf
Cook, Jonathan	grocer	57 East bay
Cook, Thomas	shopkeeper	99 King street
Cook, William	merchant	2 Gillon street
Cookson & Williamson	grocer	69 East bay
Corbett, Thomas	merchant	11 Cumberland street
Corre, Charles Godfrey	merchant	43 Broad street
Course, Isaac	merchant	98 Queen street
Crafts, William	merchant	16 East bay
Crafts, William	merchant *dw.*	12 Church street
Cramer, Tobias	shopkeeper	2 Unity alley
Crawford, William	grocer	121 Tradd street
Cripps, John Splatt	merchant	102 Broad street
Crocker & Sturgis	merchants	8 Champney's wharf
Cross, George	merchant	52 King street
Crowley, Charles	storekeeper	71 King street
Crowley, Michael	storekeeper	97 Queen street
Cruger, Frederick D.	factor	38 Meeting street
Cunningham, John	shopkeeper	146 King street
Curling, Thomas	shopkeeper	2 Cock lane
Curry, William	shopkeeper	Beale's wharf
Dacosta, Isaac	storekeeper	72 King street
Dacosta, Samuel	shopkeeper	Motte's wharf
Dallas, Angus	storekeeper	1½ Queen street
Darrell, Edward	merchant	25 East bay
Davis, Thomas	shopkeeper	207 King street

Names	*Occupations*	*Addresses*
Deady, Thomas	shopkeeper	12 Union street continued
Decker, William & Co.	merchants	8 Elliot street
Delcor, Peter	shopkeeper	24 Archdale street
Delyon, Isaac	shopkeeper	58 King street
Dennis, Richard	merchant	11 Hasell street
Desaussure, Daniel	merchant	249 Meeting street
Dewees, William	factor	101 East bay
Dodsworth, Ralph	merchant	228 King street
Dollaghan & Brannen	shopkeeper	21 East bay
Dorman, Robert	shopkeeper	26 King street
Doughty, Thomas	factor	59 Meeting street
Douglas, Joseph	shopkeeper	79 King street
Douglas, Nathaniel	shopkeeper	97 Church street
Downe, James	wharfinger	112 Church street
Duffy, Andrew	shopkeeper	238 Meeting street
Dullas, Joseph	shopkeeper	35 East bay
Duncan, Patrick	shopkeeper	80 King street
Duntze, Gerard	shopkeeper	249 King street
Dwight, Isaac	factor	Pitt street
Eames, Martha	shopkeeper	Greenwood's wharf
Edwards, Edward & Co.	grocers	17 Tradd street
Edwards, James	factor	118 Tradd street & Eveleigh's wharf
Edwards, John	shopkeeper	303 King street
Ewing, Adam	merchant	259 Meeting street
Ewing, Robert	merchant	125 Tradd street
Fabre & Price	merchants	23 East bay
Fair, William	factor	62 Meeting street
Fardo, George	factor	90 East bay
Fell, Thomas	merchant	23 Broad street
Fiddy, William	storekeeper	16 Broad street
Fields, John	tobacconist	187 Meeting street
Fisher & Berney	merchants	9 Tradd street
Fitzhipps, John	shopkeeper	155 King street
Fitzpatrick, John	merchant	14 Beresford street
Flin, Joseph	shopkeeper	31 Union street
Fluitt, Samuel	shopkeeper	1 King street
Forrest, George	merchant	67 East bay
Foskey, Bryan	shopkeeper	16 Union street
Foster, Thomas	factor	10 Meeting street
Frazer, ___	shopkeeper	220 King street
Frink, Thomas & Co.	storekeepers	Beale's wharf
Frish, Charles	shopkeeper	239 King street
Frish & Wesinger	shopkeepers	22 Union street
Fullam, William	shopkeeper	Jervey's wharf
Gabel & Corre	merchants	43 Broad street
Gadsden, Philip	factor	5 Front str. - Anson-

Names	Occupations	Addresses
		borough
Gadsden, Thomas	factor	6 Front str. - Anson borough
Galway, Michael	shopkeeper	206 King street
Gardner, John	merchant	6 Tradd street
Garrett, Joshua	merchant	George street
Geddes, Henry	storekeeper	86 King street
Gennerick, John F.	grocer	114 Tradd street
George, Henry	shopkeeper	216 King street
Gervais, John Lewis	merchant	71 Broad street
Gilbert, Elizabeth	shopkeeper	125 Church street
Gilchrist, Adam	merchant	43 East bay
Gilchrist, Malcolm	shopkeeper	Greenwood's wharf
Gist, W. Henry	shopkeeper	206 King street
Gist, William	shopkeeper	211 King street
Godfrey, Thomas	shopkeeper	154 King street
Gordon, James	merchant	6 Hasell street
Gordon, John	factor	6 Society street
Graeser, Jacob Conrad	merchant	42 Broad street
Graff & Co.	merchants	206 3/4 King street
Graham, Richard	shopkeeper	4 Union street
Grant, Hary	merchant	12 East bay
Grant, Lewis	shopkeeper	13 Union street
Gray, Benjamin	factor	77 Meeting street
Green, William	shopkeeper	71 Cock lane
Greenland, Daniel	factor	39 Meeting street
Greenland, George	factor	142 King street
Greenwood, William	merchant	1 Gadsden's alley
Greenwood, William	merchant	2 Ellery street
Gregorie son & Davidson	merchants	129 Tradd street
Grierson, James	shopkeeper	Motte's wharf
Griggs, John	factor	22 King street
Griggs, John	factor	Eveleigh's wharf
Grimes, Mary	shopkeeper	15 Union street
Hall, Daniel	merchant	3 State house square
Hamilton, James	merchant	11 Broad street
Hamilton & Harper	merchants	15 Elliot street
Harboroskie, Ann	storekeeper	46 Broad street
Hare, Edward	shopkeeper	106 King street
Hargreaves, Josh. & Jos.	merchants	21 Broad street
Harper, Robert	shopkeeper	88 King street
Harris, Andrew	merchant	6 Clifford street
Harrison, Isaac	shopkeeper	132 Queen street
Hart, Christopher	storekeeper	43 Broad street
Hart, Philip	broker	136 Queen street
Hart, Simon	shopkeeper	252 King street
Harth, ___	shopkeeper	65 East bay

Names	*Occupations*	*Addresses*
Harth, John	storekeeper	16 Archdale street
Harvey, Thomas	storekeeper	39 Archdale street
Harvey & Dill	grocers	9 Bedon's alley
Hazlehurst, Rob. & Co.	merchants	13 East bay
Henning, John Fred.	storekeeper	32 Church street
Henry, Jacob	shopkeeper	53 King street
Hilagers, George A.	shopkeeper	54 Tradd street
Hill, Paul	shopkeeper	1 Beresford street
Hillegas, Philip	grocer	96 Tradd street
Hilligas, Jacob	shopkeeper	6 Moore street
Hinson, Thomas	merchant	26 Society street
Hislop & Snowden	storekeeper	134 Queen street
Hollaway & Thayer	shopkeepers	57 King street
Horton, Thomas	shopkeeper	26 Queen street
Hostige, John	shopkeeper	Greenwood's wharf
House, Mary Ann	shopkeeper	251 King street
Howard, Robert	factor	Jervey's wharf
Howard, Robert	factor	128 Queen street
Hubert, Barry	shopkeeper	7 Union street
Hubert, Charles	merchant	27 Elliot street
Hugeley, John	shopkeeper	Smith's lane
Hunter, E. & Jacob	shopkeepers	East bay
Hymes, Solomon	shopkeeper	244 King street
Jacobs, Jacob	shopkeeper	82 King street
Jennings & Woddrop	merchants	9 East bay
Jermain, John	shopkeeper	275 King street
Jervey, Thomas	factor	1 St. Michael's alley
Jesse, Sarah	shopkeeper	50 Broad street
Jessum, Matthew	shopkeeper	137 Queen street
Johnston, Charles	merchant	Lamboll's lane
Johnston, David	shopkeeper	Greenwood's wharf
Jones, Abraham	shopkeeper	41 Church street
Jones, Alexander	shopkeeper	107 Church street
Jones, Henry	shopkeeper	Beale's wharf
Jones, Joseph	shopkeeper	15 Tradd street
Jones, Samuel	shopkeeper	268 King street
Jones, Sarah	shopkeeper	13 Beresford's alley
Joseph, Israel	indigo broker	56 King street
Keeley, Sebastian	merchant	41 East bay
Keith & Wish	shopkeeper	131 Queen street
Kelly, John	shopkeeper	116 King street
Kemmell, Mary	shopkeeper	42 Queen street
Kempton, Ann	shopkeeper	17 Chalmer's alley
Kennan, Henry	factor	1 West street
Kennear, Alexander	shopkeeper	Greenwood's wharf
Kennedy, Andrew	merchant	37 King street
Kennedy, John	shopkeeper	East bay

Names	Occupations	Addresses
Kennedy & Parker	merchants	9 Broad street
Kern, Frederick John	merchant	193 King street
Kerr, Andrew	merchant	135 Tradd street
Kersey, William	shopkeeper	184 Meeting street
Kevan & Powrie	merchant	14 Broad street
King, Eleanor	shopkeeper	45 King street
King, Timothy	shopkeeper	132 Queen street
Kirk, John	shopkeeper	Boundary street
Kirk, John	merchant	59 East bay
Lahisse, Maurice	shopkeeper	76 King street
Lamb & Montgomerie	merchant	17 Elliot street
La Motte, James	factor	Graeme's wharf
Lanchester, Henry	merchant	4 Pinckney street
Langstaff, John	storekeeper	Beale's wharf
Lawry, John	shopkeeper	14 Union street continued
Lazarus, Mark	shopkeeper	101 King street
Lee, Francis	shopkeeper	19 Tradd street
Lee & Banks	merchants	47 King street
Legare, Samuel	merchant	101 Church street
Legare, Solomon	factor	18 Friend street
Legare & Theus	merchants	101 Church street
Lepoole, Peter	merchant	82 Queen street
Leslie, George	shopkeeper	94 Church street
Levi, Hiram	broker	231 King street
Levi, Moses	shopkeeper	233 King street
Levi, Moses	shopkeeper	113 King street
Levi, Solomon	shopkeeper	247 King street
Limehouse, Thomas	shopkeeper	34 Broad street
Lindsay, Robert	merchant	136 Church street
Lloyd, John, jun.	merchant	110 Broad street
Lloyd, Joseph	shopkeeper	15 Bedon's alley
Lloyd, Joseph	shopkeeper	61 Meeting street
Lockey, George	merchant	79 East bay
Lockwood, Joshua	merchant	42 East bay
Logan, William	factor	292 King street
Lothrop, Seth	merchant	136 East bay
Love, John	fruitstand	8 Tradd street
Loveday, John	factor	10 Moore street
Luyton, William	shopkeeper	133 Tradd street
M'Bride, James	shopkeeper	58 East bay
M'Bride, Thomas	shopkeeper	24 Queen street
M'Callum, James	merchant	6 Elliot street
M'Caully & Davis	merchants	13 Broad street
M'Clure, Cochran & W.	merchants	7 Tradd street
M'Cormick, Sparks & Co.	storekeepers	183 King street
M'Crady, Edward	vinter	63 East bay
M'Credie, David	merchant	8 Broad street

Names	Occupations	Addresses
M'Donald, Charles	storekeeper	186 Meeting street
M'Donald, William	shopkeeper	22 East bay
M'Dowell, John	merchant	4 Broad street
M'Gee, John	shopkeeper	224 King street
M'Hugo, Anthony	shopkeeper	63 Meeting street
M'Kee, Samuel	shopkeeper	47 King street
M'Kenzie, Alexander	shopkeeper	12 Union street
M'Kenzie, Andrew	grocer	108 Broad street
M'Leish, Agnes	shopkeeper	1 Elliot street
M'Leod, Wm. and Co.	merchants	11 East bay
M'Mahan, John	shopkeeper	39 Queen street
M'Neal, Archibald	shopkeeper	205 Meeting street
M'Neil, Catharine	shopkeeper	37 Hasell street
M'Pherson, Duncan	shopkeeper	74 King street
M'Pherson, Jane	shopkeeper	32 King street
M'Queen, John	merchant	17 Broad street
M'Queen, Robert	shopkeeper	8 Queen street
M'Whann, William	merchant	38 Church street
Main, William	shopkeeper	71 East bay
Malcolm, Joseph	shopkeeper	East bay
Mann, Spencer	merchant	55 Church street
Mann & Foltz	merchants	3 East bay
Manson, John	merchant	38 Queen street
Markley, Abraham	shopkeeper	125 King street
Marks, Anthony	shopkeeper	218 King street
Marks, James	shopkeeper	Beale's wharf
Marshall, William	factor & wharf.	Roper's wharf
Martin, Jacob	merchant	214 Meeting street
Martin, Thomas	factor & grocer	11 Tradd street
Matthews, George	factor	102 Church street
Mayer, G. John	grocer	52 East bay
Mey, Charles Florian	merchant	40 Pinckney street
Milander, Adam	shopkeeper	64 King street
Miller, George	shopkeeper	22 Beresford street
Miller, James	merchant	103 Church street
Miller, James	wine merchant	64 East bay
Miller, John	shopkeeper	186 King street
Minchin, John	grocer	10 Elliot street
Minnick, John	merchant	32 East bay
Minott, John	factor	Lynch's lane
Mitchell, Andrew	shopkeeper	103 Meeting street
Moncrieff, John & Co.	merchants	18 Elliot street
Moodie, Benjamin	merchant	3 Church street
Moore, John	shopkeeper	190 King street
Moore, Joseph	shopkeeper	100 East bay
Morris, Thomas	merchant	14 East bay
Moses, Abraham	shopkeeper	East bay

Names	Occupations	Addresses
Moses, Henry	shopkeeper	55 East bay
Moses, Isaac	shopkeeper	2 Beresford street
Moses, Lyon	shopkeeper	83 King street
Motte, Abraham	factor	18 Meeting street
Motte, Francis	factor	66 East bay
Mulligan, Francis	shopkeeper	127 East bay
Munro, John	wharfinger	1 Pinckney street
Murphy, James	shopkeeper	25 Meeting street
Murset, Amelia	shopkeeper	27 Church street
Nelson, George	merchant	95 Church street
Newman, Fred. George	broker	11 Moore street
Nicholson, John Paul	shopkeeper	44 Union street
Nielson, James	merchant	29 Beaufain street
Norris, Nicholas	grocer	50 Broad street
Norris, Robert and Co.	factors	1 Bedon's alley
North, Edward	shipchandler	7 Church street
North and Vesey	shipchandlers	38 East bay
Oakman, Henry	merchant	16 Elliot street
O'Brian, Thomas	shopkeeper	130 Queen street
O'Hara, Daniel	merchant	128 Broad street
O'Hear, James	factor	Eveleigh's wharf
O'Hear, James	factor *dw. b.*	5 Church street continued
Osgood & Greenwood	grocers	123 Broad street
Owen, John	merchant	27 Tradd street
Patrick, Casimer	shopkeeper	185 King street
Paul, Andrew	shopkeeper	51 Church street
Payne, William	merchant	2_1 Elliot street
Peace, Isaac	merchant	110 Tradd street
Peckham, Benjamin	storekeeper	Motte's wharf
Penman, James Ed. &	merchants	75 East bay
Peppin, Joseph & Co.	merchants	35 Elliot street
Peppin, Matthew	merchant	106 Broad street
Philips, Benjamin	shopkeeper	115 King street
Plunkett, Thomas	shopkeeper	East bay
Pollock, Solomon	horsedealer	Bull & Rutledge streets
Prestman & Calhoun	merchants	136 East bay
Price, William	merchant	2 Bedon's alley
Prioleau, Samuel, jun.	factor	48 Church street
Ranger, Jacob	shopkeeper	226 King street
Reed, George	shopkeeper	2 Tradd street
Reid, George	merchant	Meeting street
Reil, George	shopkeeper	27 Henry street
Richardson, John	factor	36 Elliot street
Roberts, William	shopkeeper	4 Queen street
Robertson, Alexander	shopkeeper	95 King street
Robinson, William	merchant	26 Elliot street
Roche, Jeremiah	shopkeeper	East bay

Names	*Occupations*	*Addresses*
Rogers, Lewis	perfumer	121 Broad street
Rogers, Sarah	shopkeeper	126 Church street
Rogley, Anthony	shopkeeper	20 Tradd street
Ross, Elizabeth	shopkeeper	16 Bedon's alley
Ross, Kenneth	shopkeeper	15 Church street
Russell, Nathaniel	merchant	16 East bay
Ryan, Peter	shopkeeper	54 East bay
Sasportas, Abraham	merchant	454 East bay
Schmidt & Molich	merchant	9 Champney's wharf
Scott, James	grocer	49 East bay
Scott, Wm. & Samuel	merchants	213 King street
Selbey, George	storekeeper	220 King street
Shields, Edward	merchant	16 Tradd street
Shifflee, George	shopkeeper	18 Chalmer's alley
Shirras, Alexander	ironmonger	48 East bay
Shirtliff, Austin & Strobel	merchants	19 Broad street
Shoolbred & Moodie	merchants	26 East bay
Shultz, Casper C.	merchant	87 Broad street
Sickels, Ethan	shopkeeper	37 East bay
Simons, Anthony	factor	286 King street
Simons, Samuel	shopkeeper	43 Tradd street
Simons, Blake & Vanderhorst	factors	51 East bay
Skrine, William	factor	21 King street
Smerdon, Elias	merchant	93 King street
Smith, Andrew	shopkeepers	165 Meeting street
Smith, Archibald	shopkeeper	218 Meeting street
Smith, Desaussure & Darrel	merchants	25 East bay
Smith, George	merchant	2 Meeting street
Smith, James	shopkeeper	27 King street
Smith, John	shopkeeper	19½ Union street
Smith, John	shopkeeper	236 King street
Smith, John	merchant	15 Broad street
Smith, Josiah	merchant	2 Meeting street
Smith, Roger	merchant	43 Church street
Smith, Samuel	merchant	2 Meeting street
Smith, Whiteford	shopkeeper	1 Queen street
Smith, William	merchant	3 Broad street
Smyth, Robert	wine merchant	19 Queen street
Snowden, Charles	merchant	61 East bay
Somersall, William	merchant	2 East bay
Spaving, Patrick	shopkeeper	45 Queen street
Speisegger, John, jun.	musick shop	97 Tradd street
Spencer, George	shopkeeper	133 King street
Spitzer, Barend Moses	broker	2 Champney's row
Stevens, William	broker	154 Tradd street
Stewart, Allan	shopkeeper	68 Meeting street
Stewart, Ann	shopkeeper	29 King street

Names	*Occupations*	*Addresses*
Stewart, Thomas	merchant	29 East bay
Stewart & Potter	merchants	131 Tradd street
Stromer, H. M.	merchant	20 Elliot street
Summers, Benjamin	shopkeeper	6 Ellery street
Surtil, Martha	shopkeeper	6 Broad street
Sutherland, Francis	shopkeeper	3½ Queen street
Swinton, Hugh	factor	3 Champney's wharf
Syms, John	shopkeeper	140 Queen street
Taylor, Bennet	merchant	18 Broad street
Taylor, James	merchant	40 East bay
Teasdale, Isaac	merchant	122 Queen street
Teasdale, John	merchant	2 Champney's wharf
Teasdale, John	merchant	46 Church street
Tew, Charles	grocer	95 Tradd street
Thayer, Bartlett & Co.	merchants	31 East bay
Theus, James	merchant	89 Church street
Thomas, John B.	shopkeeper	Motte's wharf
Thompson, Daniel	shopkeeper	South bay
Thompson, Esther	shopkeeper	19 East bay
Tobias, Joseph	storekeeper	203 King street
Todd, Joseph	merchant	3 St. Michael's alley
Tonge, Mark	shopkeeper	56 East bay
Trenholm, William	merchant	1 Tradd street
Trezevant, Peter	merchant	3 Kinloch court
Tunno, Adam & Willm	merchants	28 East bay
Tunno, George	merchant	31 Broad street
Turpin, William	storekeeper	172 King street
Vale, John David	merchant	111 Broad street
Vanrynn, Emelina	storekeeper	33 Broad street
Ver Cnocke, F. I.	merchant	30 East bay
Vesey, Joseph	ship chandler	281 King street
Villepontoux, Benj.	factor	5 East bay
Virgin, George	shopkeeper	43 Tradd street
Vos, Andrew	merchant	31 Broad street
Wagner, John	merchant	85 Broad street
Walcot, Samuel	shopkeeper	60 King street
Walkman, Mark	shopkeeper	Fish market wharf
Wallace, James	merchant	1 Longitude lane
Warham, Charles	merchant	1 Gibbes's street
Waring, Thomas	factor	Jervey's wharf
Watson, Alexander	factor	107 East bay
Webb, John	merchant	14 Moore street
Wells, Edgar	merchant	10 Broad street
White, Sims & Son	factor	1 Gillon street
White, William	factor	1 Bendon's alley
Whitefield & Brown	merchants	127 Broad street
Whitesides, Edward	shopkeeper	28 Pinckney street

Names	Occupations	Addresses
Wightman, William	merchant	227 Meeting street
Wilkie, William	factor	27 East bay
Williamson, John	merchant	141 East bay
Willson, John and Co.	merchants	East bay
Wilson, Archibald	shopkeeper	253 Queen street
Withers, John	factor	29 Trott street
Woolf, Frederick	shopkeeper	8 Beresford's alley
Woolf, Henry	shopkeeper	129 King street
Woolf, Rachel	shopkeeper	41 King street
Wray, John	merchant	10 Tradd street
Wrench, Richard	shopkeeper	50 King street
Young, Hugh	merchant	96 Church street
Young, P. William	stationer	24 Broad street
Zylstra, Peter	shopkeeper	31 Elliot street

1794

Names	Occupations	Addresses
Aaron, Solomon	shopkeeper	46 King street
Abendanone, Joseph	factor	263 King street
Abrahams, Jacob	shopkeeper	70 East bay
Abrahams, Moses	shopkeeper	44 Queen street
Akin, Thomas	shopkeeper	30 Pinckney street
Alexander, David & Co.	merchants	9 Broad street
Alexander, Hector	shopkeeper	19 East bay
Alexander, William	shopkeeper	76 King street
Alexander & Price	merchants	9 Broad street
Allen & Ewing	merchants	120 Tradd street
Ancrum, William	merchant	Ellery street
Anderson, Robert	shopkeeper	19 Tradd street
Anthony, John	tobacconist	68 King street
Armstrong, Fleetwood	shopkeeper	East bay continued
Baill, John	shopkeeper	24 Union street
Baird, Thomas	shopkeeper	91 East bay
Baker, Samuel	grocer	18 Tradd street
Ball, Thomas	factor	14 Lynch's lane
Banks, Charles & Co.	merchants	22 Elliott street
Banks, Charles & Co.	merchants	129 Tradd street
Barre, Solomon	shopkeeper	65 King street
Bayer, J. G.	shopkeeper	179 Meeting street
Beatty, Robert	storekeeper	27 Broad street
Bell, David & George	merchants	20 Elliott street
Bell, William	grocer	248 King street
Bernes, Christian	shopkeeper	45 King street

Names	Occupations	Addresses
Berney, John & Co.	merchants	24 East bay
Berry, Francis H.	shopkeeper	Union street
Bithouse, John	shopkeeper	156 King street
Black, John	merchant	12 Broad street
Blackaller, Oliver	shopkeeper	6 Union continued
Blacklock, William	merchant	106 Broad street
Blake, Edward	factor	10 Legare street
Blake, John	grocer	37 East bay
Blake, John	factor	Legare street
Blakeley, Samuel	storekeeper	28 Broad street
Bold, Rhodes & Co.	merchants	132 Tradd street
Booner, Christian	shopkeeper	11 Queen street
Border, Mary	shopkeeper	15 Clifford's alley
Bourdeaux, Daniel	merchant	22 Beaufain street
Boyerle, Frederick	shopkeeper	40 Union street
Bradford & Co.	music store	31 Church street
Bradford, Charles & Co.	grocers	120 Queen street
Brailsford, John	factor	Wentworth street
Brailsford, Samuel	merchant	1 Friend street
Brodie, Thomas	factor	Pritchard's wharf
Brooke, Charles	shopkeeper	18 Union continued
Brown, James	grocer	242 King street
Brownlee, John	merchant	208 King street
Bruce, Daniel	storekeeper	25 Church street
Bryan, Arthur	merchant	17 Elliott street
Bulgin, James	merchant	11 Tradd street
Bulow, Joachim	storekeeper	119 King street
Burgess, James & Co.	merchants	23 Bay
Burn, John	shopkeeper	36 Union street
Burrel, Ebenezer	shopkeeper	Crafts wharf
Buyck, Peter	bottle seller	27 Elliott street
Byrne, Robert	shopkeeper	103 Queen street
Caldwell & Lander	grocers	215 Meeting street
Calhoun, William	merchant	99 Meeting street
Calwell, Henry, jun.	shopkeeper	20 Tradd street
Calwell, Henry, sen.	grocer	107 Church street
Cameron, Alexander	shopkeeper	81 King street
Cameron, Lewis	merchant	137 Tradd street
Canter, Jacob & Eman.	shopkeepers	18 King street
Cantor & Co.	broker	57 Church street
Canty, Henry & Co.	merchants	36 East bay
Cape, Brian	factor	80 East bay
Carpenter, James	shopkeeper	Union continued
Carr & Firby	shopkeepers	42 East bay
Carson, James	shopkeeper	67 East bay
Cart, John	factor	1 George street
Charles, Andrew	grocer	130 Broad street

Names	*Occupations*	*Addresses*
Chevers, Alexander	shopkeeper	96 King street
Chion, Peter G. & son	merchants	39 East bay
Chitty, Ann	shopkeeper	114 King street
Christie, Edward	storekeeper	93 Church street
Clarke, John	shopkeeper	122 Church street
Cochran, Robert	shopkeeper	250 King street
Cochran, Thomas	factor	Cochran's wharf
Coffin, Ebenezer	merchant	14 Tradd street
Cohen, Gershon	factor, &c	12 Orange street
Cohen, Jacob, junior	shopkeeper	91 King street
Cohen, Mordecai	shopkeeper	226 King street
Cohen, Moses	shopkeeper	191 King street
Condy, Jeremiah	merchant	217 Meeting street
Condy, Jeremiah & Co.	merchants	East bay
Cook, Jonathan	shopkeeper	122 King street
Corbett, Thomas	merchant	11 Cumberland street
Corbett, Thomas & son	merchants	East bay
Corre & Schepler	merchants	76 East bay
Couie, John	grocer	126 Broad street
Courtney, Edward	shopkeeper	173 Meeting street
Courtney, Humphrey	merchant	44 Meeting street
Crafts, William	merchant	23 Hasell street
Crafts, Wm. & Ebenezer	merchants	East bay
Crawley, George S.	shopkeeper	256 King street
Crawley, Michael	shopkeeper	235 King street
Cripps, John Splatt	merchant	102 Broad street
Crocker & Sturges	merchants	99 Church street
Cross, George	merchant	38 Tradd street
Cross & Crawley	merchants	41 East bay
Cruger, David Frederick	factor	38 Meeting
Cunaghar, Thomas	shopkeeper	Church & Water streets
Cunningham, John	shopkeeper	145 King street
Curling, Thomas	shopkeeper	199 King street
Dacosta, Isaac	merchant	91 King street
Dacosta, Joseph	broker	122 Broad street
Darrell, Edward	merchant	24 East bay
Davidson, Gilbert & J.	merchants	8 Broad street
Davis, Jane	shopkeeper	308 King street
Davis, John Maynard	insuran. broker	16 Elliott street
Davis, Thomas	shopkeeper	11 Tradd street
Dawson, John	shopkeeper	109 King street
Dazivido, Isaac	shopkeeper	71 King street
Deady, Thomas	shopkeeper	18 East bay
Dearlon, Martin	shopkeeper	45 Union street
Desaussure, Daniel	merchant	249 Meeting street
Desaussure & Greaves	factors	Crafts' wharf
Deveaux, Jacob	factor	2 St. Michaels alley

Names	Occupation	Addresses
Deveaux, Jacob & son	factors	Graeme's wharf
Dewees, William	factor	65 Meeting street
Dill, Joseph, junior	merchant	97 Church street
Dodsworth, Ralph	merchant	15 Elliott street
Dorrill, Robert	shopkeeper	6 Pinckney street
Doughty, Thomas	factor	59 Meeting street
Douglass, Nat. & John	storekeepers	94 Church street
Down, James	factor	16 East bay
Duffy, Andrew	shopkeeper	238 Meeting street
Duffy, James	shopkeeper	Market square
Dulles, Joseph	storekeeper	35 East bay
Edwards, James	factor	109 Tradd street
Ehrick & Reynolds	grocers	118 Tradd street
English, Thomas	shopkeeper	4 Tradd street
Ewing, Adam	merchant	259 Meeting street
Ewing, Robert & Adam	merchants	125 Tradd street
Fabert, Joseph	grocer	134 Queen street
Fair, William	factor	62 Meeting street
Fiddy, William	storekeeper	121 Broad street
Fields, John	tobacconist	186 Meeting street
Fields, William Brown	tobacconist	184 Meeting street
Fisher, James	merchant	16 South bay
Flemming, Robert	shopkeeper	117 King street
Flint, Joseph	grocer	31 Union street
Forrest, George	merchant	114 Broad street
Freeman, William	factor	6 South bay
Frink, Thomas & Co.	grocers	Beal's wharf
Frish, Charles	shopkeeper	188 King street
Gadsden, Philip	factor	5 Front Ansonb.
Gaillard, Theodore	factor	87 East bay
Geddis, Henry	shopkeeper	86 King street
Geddis, Robert & Co.	storekeepers	53 East bay
Gennerick, John Fred.	shopkeeper	40 Tradd street
George, Mary	shopkeeper	216 King street
Geyer, John	factor	11 Meeting street
Gilchrist, Adam	merchant	21 Church street
Gist, William	shopkeeper	209 King street
Gondeville, ___	shopkeeper	3 Union street
Gordon, James	merchant	26 East bay
Gordon, John	factor	Quince street
Gordon, Thomas	grocer	68 Meeting street
Gould, John	shopkeeper	192 King street
Graeser, Conrad Joseph	merchant	71 Meeting street
Graff, Seibels & Co.	merchants	206 King street
Graham, Samuel	merchant	
Graves, Charles	factor	79 Tradd street
Green, William	shopkeeper	73 East bay

Names	Occupations	Addresses
Greenland, George	factor	39 Meeting street
Greenwood, Robert	shopkeeper	3 Berresford street
Greenwood, Wm., junior	merchant	2 Ellery street
Greenwood, Wm., senior	merchant	28 Meeting street
Gregorie, James & son	merchants	116 Broad street
Grierson, James	shopkeeper	67 King street
Guirey, Elizabeth	shopkeeper	40 Church street
Haith, John	shopkeeper	1 Archdale street
Hall, Daniel	factor	3 State house square
Hamilton, James	merchant	11 Broad street
Hammilon, John	shopkeeper	29 Union street
Hargreaves, Joshua & J.	merchants	21 Broad street
Harris, Andrew	broker	44 Tradd street
Hart, Christian	storekeeper	204 King street
Hart, Daniel	storekeeper	56 East bay
Hart, Philip	stock-jobber	136 Queen street
Harth, John	shopkeeper	1 Archdale street
Harvey, Robert	merchant	35 Elliott street
Hawter, Elias	shopkeeper	203 King street
Hazard, Rowland	merchant	1 Pinckney street
Hazard & Robinson	merchants	6 Champney's row
Hazlehurst, Robert	merchant	14 East bay
Henry, Jacob	shopkeeper	211 King street
Hill, Thomas	grocer	9 Tradd street
Hillegas, George	shopkeeper	52 Tradd street
Hillegas, Philip	shopkeeper	96 Tradd street
House, Samuel	broker	7 Chamber's alley
Hrabowski (*sic*), Ann	storekeeper	45 Broad street
Hunter, William	shopkeeper	169 King street
Hutchinson, John	shopkeeper	65 East bay
Hutson, Abel	shopkeeper	131 Queen street
Hyams, Solomon	shopkeeper	190 King street
Hyslop, Robert	shopkeeper	63 Church street
Jacks, James	jeweller	112 Broad street
Jacobs, Samuel	shopkeeper	168 King street
Jaffray, James	merchant	135 Tradd street
Jarman, John	shopkeeper	275 King street
Jeffey, Sarah	shopkeeper	50 Broad street
Jennings & Woddrop	merchants	9 East bay
Johnson, John	storekeeper	165 King street
Johnston, James	shopkeeper	220 King street
Jones, Abraham	shopkeeper	201 King street
Jones, Alexander	grocer	106½ Church street
Jones, Joseph	shopkeeper	15 Tradd street
Jones, Samuel	shopkeeper	268 King street
Jones & Clarke	merchants	East bay
Josephs, Israel	indigo broker	262 King street

Names	Occupations	Addresses
Juvignes, Dominick	shopkeeper	18 Queen street
Kalckoffin, John	shopkeeper	88 King street
Kay & M'Cawly	grocers	2 Tradd street
Keill, John	shopkeeper	27 King street
Kelly, Mary	shopkeeper	116 King street
Kelly, Tarence	shopkeeper	44 Union street
Kempton, Ann	shopkeeper	218 King street
Kennedy, Andrew	shopkeeper	3 Union continued
Kennedy, John	shopkeeper	20 East bay
Kennedy, William	shopkeeper	4 Broad street
Kern, John Frederick	merchant	193 King street
Kerr, Andrew	merchant	8½ Broad street
Kershaw, Charles	merchant	113 Queen street
Keyan, William	merchant	136 Tradd street
King, Eleanor	shopkeeper	6 Charles street
Kirk & Lukens	merchants	59 East bay
Kohne, John Frederick	merchant	Crafft's (*sic*) wharf
Kripps, Andrew	shopkeeper	King street
Lamb & Montgomery	merchants	23 East bay
Lamotte, James	factor	12 Church street
Lamotte & Chisonn	factors	Vanderhorst's wharf
Lanchester, Henry	grocer	3 Pinckney street
Lange, J. H.	merchant	133 Tradd street
Langstaff, John	merchant	6 Elliott continued
Lathauson & Co.	shopkeepers	23 Union street
Lazarus, Mark	shopkeeper	101 King street
Lee, John & William	merchants	47 King street
Lee, Stephen	factor	42 Broad street
Lee & Miles	factors	Geyer's wharf
Legare, Samuel	merchant	101 Church street
Legare, Solomon	factor	5 East bay
Legare, Theus, & Prioleau	merchants	131 Broad street
Legge, James	shopkeeper	198 King street
Lenox, William & Co.	merchants	120 Broad street
Leslie & Campbell	shopkeepers	96 Church street
Levy, Hart	shopkeeper	184 King street
Levy, Lyon	shopkeeper	204 King street
Levy, Moses C.	shopkeeper	283 King street
Levy, Nathan	shopkeeper	222 King street
Levy, Samuel	shopkeeper	182 King street
Levy, Solomon	shopkeeper	247 King street
Lewers, Thomas	shopkeeper	200 King street
Ley, Francis	shopkeeper	Elliott street
Liddle, John	shopkeeper	South bay
Limehouse, Robert	shopkeeper	34½ Broad street
Lindsay, Robert	merchant	South bay point
Littlejohn, Duncan	merchant	140 Church street

Names	Occupations	Addresses
Lloyd, Joseph	shopkeeper	13 Elliott street
Lloyd & Paterson	merchants	31 Broad street
Lothrop, Seth & Co.	merchants	East bay
Love, John	fruit-shop	8 Tradd street
Loveday, John	factor	10 Moore street
Luyton, William	storekeeper	8 Elliott street
Lyon, Mordecai	shopkeeper	53 East bay
Lyon, Moses	shopkeeper	153 King street
M'Beath, Alexander	merchant	105 Broad street
M'Beath & Ross	merchants	121 Tradd street
M'Bride, James	shopkeeper	58 East bay
M'Bride & Forsyth	shopkeepers	225 Meeting street
M'Clure, Cochran & W.	merchants	7 Tradd street
M'Credie, David & Co.	merchants	8 Broad street
M'Donald, Patrick	shopkeeper	125 Church street
M'Donald, William	grocer	22 East bay
M'Dowall, James	shopkeeper	58 King street
M'Dowall, John	shopkeeper	39 Queen street
M'Dowall, John	merchant	104 Broad street
M'Gee, John	shopkeeper	223 King street
M'Kenzie, Andrew	grocer	108 Broad street
M'Kenzie & Hinson	merchants	29 Broad street
M'Laren, James	shopkeeper	6 Union street
M'Pherson, Duncan	shopkeeper	74 King street
M'Queen, John	merchant	19 Broad street
M'Whann, William	merchant	38 Church street
Macauley, George	merchant	17 Broad street
Macleod, William	merchant	10 East bay
Mailone, James	shopkeeper	97 Queen street
Mame, William	grocer	71 East bay
Mann & Foltz	merchants	13 East bay
Manson, John	merchant	32 Pinckney street
Markley, Abraham	merchant	124 King street
Marks, Humphrey	shopkeeper	217 King street
Marshall, Barbary	shopkeeper	194 King street
Marshall, William	factor	6 East bay
Martin, Thomas	merchant	1 Tradd street
Martin, Davis & Martin	merchants	21 East bay
Mathews, George	merchant	102 Church street
Mayer, John George	insuran. broker	129 Broad street
Meiks, Joseph	shopkeeper	15 Union street
Mey, Florian Charles	merchant	40 Pinckney street
Meyers, Thomas	shopkeeper	66 King street
Miller, James	wine merchant	64 East bay
Miller, James	merchant	103 Church street
Miller, John	shopkeeper	186 King street
Miller & Robinson	storekeepers	17 Tradd street

Names	Occupations	Addresses
Milligan, John	retailer lumber	6 Bedon's alley
Minnick, John	merchant	Craft's wharf
Mitchell, Andrew	shopkeeper	224 Meeting street
Mitchell, Andrew	shopkeeper	105 Queen street
Mitchell, John Hinckley	merchant	10 Lynch's lane
Mitchell, John Hinckley	grocer	51 East bay
Montgomery, Thomas	merchant	23 East bay
Moore, John	shopkeeper	189 King street
Morris, Thomas	merchant	46 Trott street
Moses, Abraham & H.	shopkeepers	245 King street
Moses, Henry	shopkeeper	55 East bay
Moses, Isaac	shopkeeper	228 King street
Moses, Lyon	shopkeeper	15 Allen street
Moses, Philip	broker	14 Friend street
Mota, Isaac	shopkeeper	18 King street
Motte, Francis	merchant	18 South bay
Muir & Boyd	merchants	111 Broad street
Muncrieff, John & Co.	merchants	105 Broad street
Murphy, James	shopkeeper	27 Meeting street
Nann, Mary	shopkeeper	3 Meeting street
Nathans, Moses B.	broker	45 Queen street
Nickson, John	shopkeeper	6 Ellery street
Norris, Nicholas	broker	264 King street
North, Edward	merchant	7 Church street
North & Vesey	ship-chandlers	38 East bay
Ogier, Thomas	factor	Geyer's new buildings
O'Hara, Charles	merchant	128 Broad street
O'Hara, Daniel	merchant	128 Broad street
O'Hear, James	factor	8 Meeting street
Owen, John	merchant	27 Tradd street
Pain & Bridgham	merchants	6 Champney's W.
Parris, Francis	shopkeeper	69 East bay
Patricks, Cashmere	shopkeeper	187 King street
Patton, Alexander	shopkeeper	207 King street
Payne, William	merchant	115 Broad street
Peace, Isaac	merchant	110 Tradd street
Peirson, James	merchant	42 Broad street
Penman, J. & E. & Co.	merchants	75 East bay
Pepoon, Otis & Co.	merchants	East bay
Peppin, Joseph & Co.	merchants	32 East bay
Peter, Henry	shopkeepers	21 Elliott street
Philips, Benjamin, jun.	shopkeeper	196 King street
Pollock, Solomon	horse-dealer	7 Bull street
Potter, John	merchant	131 Tradd street
Pourie, Bazil	merchant	14 Broad street
Poyas & Foster	merchants	126 Tradd street
Presstman, William	merchant	10 East bay

Names	Occupations	Addresses
Price, John	merchant	108 Church street
Price, William	merchant	17 Elliott street
Prioleau, John	factor	15 Pinckney street
Prioleau, Samuel	factor	48 Church street
Redlech, William	broker	4 Champney's R.
Regley, Anthony	shopkeeper	24 Elliott street
Richardson, John	merchant	36 Elliott street
Roberts, William	shopkeeper	6 Queen street
Robertson, Alexander	shopkeeper	95 King street
Robertson, James	shopkeeper	197 King street
Robinson, William	shopkeeper	26 Elliott street
Rogers, Lewis	perfumer	24 Broad streeet
Rogers, Sarah	shopkeeper	126 Church street
Rose, Alexander	merchant	2 Church street
Ross, Elizabeth	shopkeeper	244 King street
Ross, Kenneth	shopkeeper	15 Church street
Rowand, Robert	merchant	2 Friend street
Rumney, Joseph	grocer	99 East bay
Russell, Nathaniel	merchant	16 East bay
Ryan, Peter Saul	shopkeeper	54 East bay
Sarazin, Jonathan	merchant	3 St. Philip's street
Sarzedas, Moses	merchant	127 Broad street
Sasportas, Abraham	merchant	16 Queen street
Schaffer, Frederick	shopkeeper	8 Berresford street
Schmidth & Molich	merchants	79 East bay
Schutt, Casper C.	merchant	87 Broad street
Scott, James	grocer	48 East bay
Selby, George	merchant	229 King street
Sheppard, Jane	shopkeeper	37 Meeting street
Shields, Edward	storekeeper	16 Tradd street
Shirrliff & Austin	merchants	45 Meeting street
Sibbins, Sibbe	shopkeeper	225 Meeting street
Sibley, Lewis	shopkeeper	6 Moore street
Simmons, Anthony	factor	285 King street
Simmons, Charles H.	broker	216 Meeting street
Simmons, Vanderhorst & Co.	factors	15 East bay
Simons, Keating	factor	2 Pinckney street
Simons, Thomas	factor	70 Meeting street
Smith, Archibald	grocer	24 Queen street
Smith, Caleb	shopkeeper	51 Church street
Smith, James	shopkeeper	43 Union street
Smith, John Christian	factor	53 King street
Smith, John Holmes	shopkeeper	35 Broad street
Smith, Julius	merchant	East bay & Gillon streets
Smith, Whitford	shopkeeper	1 Queen street
Smith, William	merchant	East bay
Smith, William	ironmonger	3 Broad street

Names	Occupations	Addresses
Smyth, John	merchant	Ellery street
Smyth, John	shopkeeper	239 King street
Snowden, Charles	merchant	67 East bay
Solomons, Hyam	shopkeeper	130 Queen street
Somersall, Thomas A.	merchant	___
Somersall, William	merchant	2 East bay
Somersall, Wm. & son	merchants	3 East bay
Spering, Patrick	shopkeeper	212 King street
Spitzer, Bernard Moses	broker	2 Champney's row
Stevens, William	indigo factor	124 Tradd street
Stewart, Thomas	merchant	29 East bay
Stewart, William	shopkeeper	Graehms
Stromer, Henry Maine	merchant	49 East bay
Sutherland, Francis	shopkeeper	4 Queen street
Sutherland, George	shopkeeper	40 Church street
Sutton, John	shopkeeper	180 Meeting street
Swinton, Hugh	indigo factor	84 Meeting street
Sylvester, Christian	shopkeeper	Crafft's (sic) wharf
Syme, John	shopkeeper	139 Queen street
Taylor, Bennet	merchant	18 Broad street
Taylor, Margaret	storekeeper	29 Elliott street
Teasdale, John	merchant	43 East bay
Teasdale & Kiddell	merchants	121 Queen street
Thayer, Ebenezer	merchant	52 Meeting street
Thayer, Williams & J.	merchants	31 East bay
Therie, John Francis	merchant	68 East bay
Theus, James	merchant	89 Church street
Theus, Samuel	vintner	25 East bay
Thomas, Francis	grocer	60 King street
Thomas, James	merchant	31 Church street
Thomas, John David	shopkeeper	26 Union street
Thomson, Daniel	shopkeeper	South bay
Tobias, Joseph	shopkeeper	202 King street
Tonge, Mark	shopkeeper	60 East bay
Trenholm, William	merchant	18 Elliott street
Trezevant, Peter	merchant	30 Queen street
Tullock, Peter	shopkeeper	2 Queen street
Tunno, Adam	merchant	28 East bay
Tunno, Thomas	merchant	22 Broad street
Tunno, William	merchant	East bay
Tunnos & Cox	merchants	28 East bay
Turpin, William	merchant	172 King street
Van Ryan & Savage	shopkeepers	33 Broad street
Vercnocke & Cockle	merchants	4 Bedon's alley
Vesey, Joseph	merchant	280 King street
Virgin, George	shopkeeper	43 Tradd street
Vos, Andrew	merchant	Society street

Names	*Occupations*	*Addresses*
Vos & Graves	merchants	17 East bay
Wadsworth & Turpin	merchants	171 King street
Wagner, George	merchant	Broad street
Wall, Richard Gilbert	vintner	36 Queen street
Waring, Thomas	factor	40 Meeting street
Watson, Alexander	factor	107 East bay
Watson, Isaac	shopkeeper	274 King street
Webb, John	merchant	14 Moore street
Welch, George	tobacconist	19 Trott street
Wells, Edgar & son	merchants	10 Broad street
White, James	shopkeeper	136 Church street
White, John	factor	12 Ellery street
White, Sims	factor	12 Ellery street
White, William & Co.	merchants	Bedon's alley
Whitfield & Brown	merchants	2 Bedon's alley
Wilkie, William	factor	11 East bay
Winthrop, Joseph	merchant	90 Tradd street
Winthrop, Joseph	merchant	East bay
Woolf, Frederick	shopkeeper	17 Union street
Woolf, Henry	shopkeeper	232 King street
Wrainch, Richard	shopkeeper	51 King street
Yates, William	shopkeeper	19 Union street
Young, Hugh	shopkeeper	96½ Church street
Young, William Price	printer, bookseller, and stationer	43 Broad street
Zealy, Mrs. ___	shopkeeper	297 King street
Zylstra, Peter	shopkeeper	31 Elliott street

Chapter III / Planters and Farmers

The production of agricultural products in the areas surrounding Charleston played a major role in economic growth of Charleston. It became fashionable for the successful Low Country planter to build a home in Charleston in addition to maintaining his plantation in the rural area near Charleston.

It is interesting to note that no one is listed as a planter or farmer in the 1782 directory. There are no farmers listed in the 1790 directory, and only one farmer is listed in the 1794 directory. There are many planters listed in the 1790 and 1794 directories.

A count of the planters and farmers is shown below.

Planters and Farmers

	1782	1790	1794
farmer			1
planter		128	98
plantress		2	

Planters and Farmers

1790

Names	Addresses	Occupations
Allston, William	planter	104 East bay
Ancrum, William	planter	13 Ellery street
Ball, John	planter	24 Hazle street
Beach, Samuel	planter	8 King street
Beekman, Bernard	planter	109 East bay
Bellenger, John	planter	65 Meeting street
Beresford, Richard	planter	75 Broad street
Beselleau, Lewis	planter	28 Beaufain street
Blake, Elizabeth	plantress	9 Church street

Names	Occupations	Addresses
Bocquet, Peter	planter	Wentworth street
Bonfell, Samuel	planter	5 Wentworth street
Bowman, John	planter	124 East bay
Brailsford, William	planter	45 Meeting street
Broughton, Ann	plantress	103 Tradd street
Brown, Joseph	planter	66 Tradd street
Brown, Samuel	planter	7 Cumberland street
Bryan, John	planter	39 Pinckney street
Bull, William	planter	282 King street
Campbell, M'Cartan	planter	105 East bay
Chisholm, Alexander	planter	307 King street
Cordes, John	planter	72 Broad street
Cox, John	planter	128 Church street
Dawson, John	planter	92½ East bay
Deas, John	planter	14 Meeting street
Deas, John, jun.	planter	Lamboll's lane
Doughty, William	planter	202 Meeting street
Elliott, Thomas	planter	3 Gibbes street
Elliott, Thomas O.	planter	17 Legare street
Evans, George	planter	44 Trott street
Eveleigh, Thomas	planter	229 Meeting street
Farr, Joseph	planter	12 Orange street
Fishburne, William	planter	12 Hasell street
Fraser, Alexander	planter	78 Tradd street
Fripp, William	planter	305 King street
Fuller, Thomas	planter	91 Tradd street
Gadsden, Christopher	planter	4 Front str. – Ansonborough
Gaillard, Theodore	planter	88 East bay
Geyer, John	planter	11 Meeting street
Gibbes, John	planter	5 Legare street
Gibbes, Robert	planter	19 Meeting street
Gillon, Alexander	planter	89 Tradd street
Glaze, John	planter	3 Cumberland street
Grimball, C. Isaac	planter	273 Meeting street
Hamilton, James	planter	53 Meeting street
Heyward, Nathaniel	planter	118 East bay
Hinlen, Thomas	planter	Bull street
Horry, Thomas	planter	274 Meeting street
Hume, John	planter	77 Queen street
Hutchinson, Thomas, jun.	planter	21 South bay
Hutchinson, Thomas, sen.	planter	East bay
Inglis, Alexander	planter	84 Queen street
Izard, Ralph	planter	83 Broad street
Jackson, John	planter	26 Guignard street
Johnston, Andrew	planter	3 St. Philip's street
Jones, Thomas	planter	4 Guignard street

Names	Occupations	Addresses
Kennedy, James	planter	100 Tradd street
Kinloch, Cleland	planter	Hasell street
Kinloch, Francis	planter	123 Queen street
Ladson, James	planter	Lamboll's lane
Lawton, Winmal	planter	Lynch's lane
Legare, Daniel	planter	Ansonborough
Legare, Daniel, jun.	planter	11 Mazyck street
Legare, Thomas	planter	50 Tradd street
Legge, Edward	planter	45 Trott street
Lehre, Thomas	planter	293 King street
Lenud, Henry	planter	1 Hasell street
Lesesne, Isaac	planter	111 East bay
Lightwood, Edward	planter	266 Meeting street
Lloyd, John	planter	8 Legare street
Lockwood, Thomas	planter	207 Meeting street
Loocock, Aaron	planter	31 Tradd street
Lowndes, Rawlins	planter	74 Broad street
M'Callister, Archibald	planter	23 Hasell street
M'Pherson, John	planter	23 Legare street
Manigault, Gabriel	planter	89 East bay
Manigault, Joseph	planter	82 Tradd street
Matthews, Benjamin	planter	108 Church street
Matthews, William	planter	92 Meeting street
Mazyck, Stephen	planter	1 Short street
Middleton, Thomas	planter	82 Tradd street
Mitchell, John	planter	264 Meeting street
Moore, John	planter	51 King street
Morris, Lewis	planter	260 Meeting street
Moultrie, William	planter	60 Meeting street
Muncreef, Richard	planter	5 Magazine street
Parker, Isaac	planter	11 Legare street
Parker, John	planter	10 George street
Pinckney, Thomas, jun.	planter	270 Meeting street
Porcher, Philip	planter	6 Archdale street
Postell, Thomas	planter	179 King street
Pringle, Robert	planter	South bay
Prioleau, Samuel	planter	21 Church street
Quash, Robert	planter	76 Broad street
Radcliffe, Thomas	planter	6 George street
Ravenel, Daniel	planter	100 Broad street
Richardson, John	planter	120 King street
Rivers, John	planter	Stoll's alley
Rivers, Thomas	planter	Stoll's alley
Roper, Thomas	planter	4 East bay
Rose, Alexander	planter	2 Church street
Sanders, John	planter	8 Cumberland street
Saunders, Roger Parker	planter	22 South bay

Names	Occupations	Addresses
Scott, William	planter	85 Tradd street
Screven, Thomas	planter	117 Church street
Simmons, Francis	planter	Legare street
Simmons, Thomas	planter	133 Church street
Simmons, William	planter	104 Tradd street
Simons, James	planter	2 Pinckney street
Simons, Thomas	planter	130 East bay
Sinkler, James	planter	32 Pinckney street
Skirving, William	planter	South bay
Smith, O'brien	planter	10 Guignard
Smith, Peter	planter	26 Beaufain street
Smith, Thomas	planter	Harleston's green
Snipes, William Clay	planter	208 King street
Stevens, Daniel	planter	41 George street
Tart, Nathan	planter	96 Queen street
Theus, Simeon	planter	277 King street
Todd, John	planter	271 Meeting street
Tweed, Alexander	planter	112 Queen street
Wainwright, Richard	planter	286 King street
Waring, Joseph	planter	69 Meeting street
Washington, William	planter	1 Church street
Weston, Plowden	planter	37 Queen street
White, Blakely	planter	36 King street
Wilkinson, Morton	planter	5 Church street
Wilson, Daniel	planter	Elliot's b. Meeting str.
Wilson, Joseph	planter	4 Church street
Wragg, John	planter	15 Union street continued
Young, William	planter	Lynch's lane

1794

Names	Occupations	Addresses
Allston, William	planter	9 King street
Ash, John, senior	planter	17 South bay
Ball, John	planter	24 Hasell
Bayly, Benjamin	planter	21 South bay
Bowman, John	planter	33 Wentworth street
Bryan, John	planter	39 Pinckney street
Bull, John	planter	316 King street
Campbell, David	planter	5 Legare street
Carson, William	planter	9 Meeting street
Champneys, John	planter	24 King street

Names	Occupations	Addresses
Chisolm, Alexander	planter	307 King street
Cox, John	planter	128 Church street
Dawson, John	planter	94 East bay
Dewar, Robert	planter	93 Tradd street
Doughty, William	planter	202 Meeting street
Douxsaint, William	planter	84 Church street
Drayton, Thomas	planter	91 Queen street
Elliott, Thomas	planter	Gibbes's street
Elliott, Thomas Odinfell	planter	18 Legare street
Filbin, Charles	planter	9 Friend street
Flagg, George	planter	Federal
Fripp, William	planter	8 Meeting street
Fuller, Thomas	planter	91 Tradd street
Gadsden, Christopher	planter	4 Front Ansonb.
Gaillard, Theodore	planter	81 East bay
Garden, Alexander	planter	3 Church street
Gibbes, John	planter	67 Tradd street
Gray, Benjamin	planter	22 Trott street
Heyward, Nathaniel	planter	118 East bay
Heyward, Thomas, jun.	planter	Church street
Heyward, Thomas, sen.	planter	88 Tradd street
Horry, Thomas	planter	274 Meeting street
Huger, Isaac	planter	59 Broad street
Huger, John	planter	73 Broad street
Izard, Ralph, junior	planter	83 Broad street
Johnston, Charles	planter	3 Lamboll street
Kennedy, James	planter	32 Wentworth street
Laughton, Winborn	planter	5 Lynch's lane
Legare, Thomas	planter	50 Tradd street
Lehre, Thomas	planter	293 King street
Lightwood, Edward	planter	266 Meeting street
Lloyd, John	planter	6 Lamboll street
Logan, William	planter	292 King street
Lowndes, Rawlins	planter	74 Broad street
M'Call, James	planter	88 Church street
M'Neale, Ralph	planter	73 Church street
M'Pherson, John	planter	27 Trott street
Managault, Joseph	planter	89 East bay
Mathews, William	planter	Kinloch court
Mazyck, Stephen, senior	planter	Short street
Mazyck, William	planter	75 Broad street
Miles, Robert	planter	10 Pinckney street
Morris, Lewis	planter	260 Meeting street
Motte, Abraham	planter	18 Meeting street
Neufville, Edward	planter	22 Legare street
Parker, John	planter	30 Trott street
Pendarvis, Josiah	planter	49 Tradd street

Names	Occupations	Addresses
Peronneau, William	planter	266 Meeting street
Perry, Edward	planter	1 Pinckney street
Petrie, Edmund	planter	82 Church street
Pinckney, Charles	planter	268 Meeting street
Pinckney, Thomas	planter	4 Price's alley
Porcher, Philip	planter	6 Archdale street
Postell, Thomas	planter	8 Friend street
Quash, Robert	planter	76 Broad street
Quin, James	planter	16 Chambers' alley
Ratcliffe, Thomas	planter	6 George street
Ravenel, Daniel	planter	100 Broad street
Revel, John	planter	80 Church street
Richardson, James	planter	121 King street
Rivers, Francis	planter	8 Amen street
Rose, Hugh	planter	1 East bay
Rutledge, John, junior	planter	56 Meeting street
Saunders, Roger Parker	planter	18½ Friend street
Scott, William	planter	17 Lynch's lane
Scrivan, Thomas	planter	117 Church street
Seabrook, Joseph	planter	304 King street
Shapple, M.	planter	21 Tradd street
Shoolbread, James	planter	15 Meeting street
Singleton, Richard	planter	Pitt street
Skirving, William	planter	1 South bay
Smith, John	planter	36 Church street
Smith, O'Brian	planter	105 Queen street
Smith, Peter	planter	26 Beaufain street
Smith, Roger	planter	2 Orange street
Smyth, Robert	planter	19 Queen street
Thomson, John	planter	9 Pinckney street
Tweed, Alexander	planter	111 East bay
Vale, John David	farmer	Cumming street
Vanderhorst, Anoldus	planter	15 East bay
Wagner, John	planter	85 Broad street
Wainwright, Richard	planter	286 King street
Warham, Charles	planter	100 Tradd street
Waring, John	planter	Federal
Washington, William	planter	1 Church street
Weston, Plowden	planter	37 Queen street
Wragg, John	planter	12 Union continued
Wragg, William	planter	86 East bay

Chapter IV / Teachers

During the eighteenth century, education in South Carolina was centered in Charleston. In the early years of the eighteenth century the Society for the Propagation of the Gospel in Foreign Parts was instrumental in the education of Charleston youth. Because of the efforts of the Society, there was a strong religious influence in education in South Carolina. In 1712 "An act for Founding and Erecting a Free School in Charles Town" was passed. Although the government had expressed an interest in education, it still remained a personal matter throughout the eighteenth century.

Schools were operated by individuals or charitable societies during the eighteenth century, and these schools supplied the major part of education. Courses of study in the classics, mathematics, and the arts were available to the students of Charleston. During the post-Revolutionary period, some of the prosperous Charleston residents continued to send their children abroad for education. Other children were educated in the local schools and in the colleges and universities which had been established in the United States.

A count of the teachers is shown below.

Teachers

	1782	1790	1794
academy		2	
boarding school		3	4
colum. acad.		1	
dancing academy			1
dancing master			1
French teacher			1
music master		1	2
proff. music		1	
school master	1	15	15

Teachers

1782

Names	Occupations	Addresses
Alexander, Alexander	schoolmaster	25 Union street Contd.

1790

Names	Occupations	Addresses
Alexander, Alexander	school-master	7 Union street continued
Baker, Samuel	school-master	10 Church street
Bradford, Thomas	proff. music	14 Elliott street
Bricken, Sarah	school-mistress	129 East bay
Colcock, Mrs. ___	board school	101 Tradd street
Connelly, Mary	school-mistress	205 Meeting street
Cox, Ann	school-mistress	10 Stoll's alley
Dickson, Samuel	school-master	72 Meeting street
Dimes, Ann	school-mistress	31 Church street
Duff, David	school-master	4 Wentworth street
Eckhard, Jacob	music master	33 Archdale street
Fogartie, Mary	school-mistress	280 King street
Forrest, Michael	school-master	4 Wentworth street
Fullerton, Elizabeth	school-mistress	86 Queen street
Good, Sarah	school-mistress	9 Stoll's alley
Hoyland, Ann Maria	school-mistress	86 Broad street
Hutchings, William	school-master	14 Hasell street
Jamieson, Rebecca	boarding sch.	29 Church street
Latham, Eleanor	school-mistress	32 Meeting street
M'Lish, Mary	school-mistress	54 Church street
Mann, Margaret	school-mistress	58 Meeting street
Nixon, Rev. William	colum. acad.	New Market
Oliver, James	school-master	22 Trott street
Osborne, Henry	academy	11 Pinckney street
Paget, Thomas	school-master	63 Church street
Pecton, Ruth	school-mistress	Wyatt's lot
Rhind, Elizabeth	boarding sch.	98 Church street
Rogers, Maria	school-mistress	St. Philip's street
Rout, George	school-master	9 Moore street
Royall, William	school-master	35 Tradd street
Smith, Rev. William		St. Philip's academy

Names	*Occupations*	*Addresses*
Shead, George	school-master	283 King street
Stewart, Jane	school-mistress	20 Union street continued
Thompson, J. Hamden	school-master	30 King street
Thompson, John	school-master	66 Meeting street
Tucker, Mary	school-mistress	9 Charles street
Ward, Theonhilus	school-master	24 Queen street
Young, Susannah	school-mistress	Lynch's lane

1794

Names	*Occupations*	*Addresses*
Akin, Ann	boarding school	76 Church street
Alexander, Alexander	school-master	4 Union continued
Andrews & Pendergrass	school-master	48 Meeting street
Cleary, John R.	school-master	12 Liberty street
Colcock, Melescent	boarding school	101 Tradd street
Dickson, Samuel	school-master	72 Meeting street
Eckhart, Jacob	music-master	4 Berresford street
Fogartie, Mary	school-mistress	12 King street
Fullerton, Elizabth	boarding school	86 Queen street
Gibson, Ann Maria	school-mistress	Pinckney street
Harvey, Elizabeth	school-mistress	3 Orange street
Hoyland, Ann Maria	school-mistress	86 Bread (*sic*) street
Hutchings, William B.	school-master	14 Hasell street
Jamieson, Rebecca	boarding school	105 East bay
Johnston, William	school-master	Stoll's alley
Labbe, Anthony	music master	23 Berresford street
Lafar, Joseph	dancing master	Chur. & Lynch's lane
Laval, Jacint	F. teacher	1 Kinloch-court
Nixon, William	school master	95 Tradd street
Osborne, Henry	school-master	78 Queen street
Pagett, Thomas	school-master	6 Cumberland street
Rout, George	school-master	9 Moore street
Royall, William	school-master	48 Tradd street
Sheed, George	school-master	283 King street
Smith, Christiana	school-mistress	10 Amen street
Stewarts, Miss ___	school-mistress	3 Kinloch-court
Tarver, John	school-master	Archadle street
Thomson, James H.	school-master	30 King street
Turner, Thomas	dancing acad.	94 Queen street

Chapter V / Tavernkeepers, Innholders, Boardinghouses, Etc.

Charleston was the center of the social and business life of the province prior to the Revolutionary War. Charleston retained that role for many years following the Revolution. Therefore, there was a necessity for inns, boarding houses, and taverns in post-Revolutionary Charleston.

The taverns were gathering places for the men. They served as a focal point for all in the community. They were a place for the exchange of information and news and served as a meeting place for clubs and committees. The tavern was a popular place on election day.

The coffeehouses were the meeting places of the merchants, businessmen, and politicians and the scene of many business transactions. Auctions were frequently held at the coffeehouses, and many real estate transactions were concluded there.

A count of the tavernkeepers, innholders, boarding houses, etc., is shown below.

Tavernkeepers, Innholders, Boardinghouses, Etc.

	1782	1790	1794
beer house		1	
billiard (*sic*) table			2	2
boardinghouse		22	29
coffeehouse		1	2
hotel			1
innholder		6	
innkeeper			1
porter house		2	1
tavernkeeper	6		5

Tavernkeepers, Innholders, Boardinghouses, Etc.

1782

Names	Occupations	Addresses
Coram, John	tavernkeeper	82 Church street
Ramadge, Mrs. ___	tavernkeeper	80 Broad street
Robertson, John	tavernkeeper	28 Bay
Stewart, Jane	tavernkeeper	22 Bay
Strickland, James	tavernkeeper	92 Broad street
Throne, Philip	tavernkeeper	43 Queen street

1790

Names	Occupations	Addresses
Bampfield, William	porter house	183 Meeting street
Boddie, Sarah	boardinghouse	26 Tradd street
Bohm, Charles	billiard (*sic*) table	38 King street
Booth, Catharine	boardinghouse	84 East bay
Bradford, Charles	porter house	130 Broad street
Christian, Robert	boardinghouse	136 Tradd street
Cohen, Moses	boardinghouse	98 King street
Dawson, Christiana	boardinghouse	2 Kinloch's court
Hand, Margarett	boarding h.	18 Queen street
Harris, Thomas	boardinghouse	237 King street
Hauser, Elias	boarding h.	205 King street
Hodson, Margaret	boardinghouse	57 King street
M'Kann, James	beer house	12 Beresford street
Manners, Archibald	boardinghouse	8 Bedon's alley
Martin, John C.	innholder	230 King street
Martin, Rebecca	boardinghouse	14 Queen street
Moubray, William	boardinghouse	112 Tradd street
Perry, Eleanor	boardinghouse	204 Meeting street
Pillason, William	billiard (*sic*) table	26 King street
Purse, Elizabeth	boardinghouse	30 Broad street
Ramage, Frances	boardinghouse	6 Cumberland street
Reese, Martha	boardinghouse	95 Queen street
Silk, Susannah	boardinghouse	22 Union street continued
Singleton, Bracey	innholder	Louisb. coffee house
Smith, Morton	inholder (*sic*)	Jervey's wharf
Stewart, Margaret	innholder	66 East bay

Names	Occupations	Addresses
Teibout, Sarah	boardinghouse	4 Kinloch court
Theus, Rosanna	boardinghouse	87 Church street
Todd, John	innholder	70 Meeting street
Turpin, Hannah	boardinghouse	53 Church street
Wallace, Elizabeth	boardinghouse	23 Union street continued
Wesner, Philip Henry	innholder	262 King street
Wilkie, William	boardinghouse	6 Bedon's alley
Williams, John	coffee-house	128 Tradd street

1794

Names	Occupations	Addresses
Beauford, Charles	billiard (*sic*) table	32 King street
Bennett, William	boardinghouse	172 Meeting street
Bochet & Co.	F. coffee house	Anson corner
Bodie, Sarah	boardinghouse	26 Tradd street
Booth, Catharine	boardinghouse	84 East bay
Bricken, Sarah	boardinghouse	6 Tradd street
Budd, Abigail	boardinghouse	46 Church street
Calvert, Elizabeth	boardinghouse	110 Queen street
Coats, Thomas	tavernkeeper	40 East bay
Dawson, Christiana	boardinghouse	2 Kinloch court
Denton, James	tavernkeeper	87 King street
Freer, Sarah	boardinghouse	107 Queen street
Galloway, John	tavernkeeper	10 Union street
Gamble, John	innkeeper	97 King street
Good, Sarah	boardinghouse	37 King street
Ham, Mrs. ___	boardinghouse	24 Berresford's alley
Harris, John Hartley	hotel	63 East bay
Harris, Thomas	boardinghouse	237 King street
Harvey, Thomas	boardinghouse	3 Market square
Hillegas, Joseph	billiard (*sic*) table	244 Meeting street
Jacks, Victor	boardinghouse	128 Queen street
Karr, James	boardinghouse	1 St. Michaels alley
Keiser, John Jacob	tavernkeeper	57 King street
Keith, Mrs. ___	boardinghouse	119 Queen street
Ladson, Mrs. ___	boardinghouse	5 Orange street
M'Cann, Edward	porter house	4 Market square
M'Clary, Jane	boardinghouse	3 Union street
M'Clish, Mrs. ___	boardinghouse	54 Church street
Martin, John Christoph.	tavernkeeper	230 King street
Nott, Isabella	boardinghouse	58 Church street

Names	Occupations	Addresses
Ramage, Mrs. Charles	boardinghouse	223 Meeting street
Shaw, Elizabeth	boardinghouse	16 Elliott street
Silk, Susanna	boardinghouse	3 Union continued
Simons, Francis	boardinghouse	9 Union continued
Smith, Mrs. ___	boardinghouse	15 Broad street
Thomas, Elizabeth	boardinghouse	10 Berresford's alley
Thomson, Elizabeth	boardinghouse	28 Church street
Turpin, Hannah	boardinghouse	21 Berresford's alley
Warnock, Joseph	boardinghouse	74½ East bay
Welch, Mary	boardinghouse	61 Meeting street
Williams, John	coffee-house	128 Tradd street

Religion was an active force in the lives of the eighteenth century residents of Charleston. This is evidenced by the many churches, the charitable societies, and advertisements in the newspapers offering religious books for sale.

The Anglican church played a prominent part in the development of religious intellectual thought in eighteenth century Charleston. In 1706 the Anglican Church was established by law in the colony. During the first half of the eighteenth century, the Society for the Propagation of the Gospel in Foreign Parts sent an educated clergy and many school masters to South Carolina. Thus the Anglican church gained a stronghold in South Carolina prior to the Revolutionary War although its members never numbered a majority of the inhabitants.

South Carolina had become home to Scotch and English Presbyterians, Independents, Congregationalists, Quakers, Baptists, Huguenots, Roman Catholics, and Jews during the first half of the eighteenth century. Although there are only two ministers, both of whom were Anglican ministers, listed in the 1782 city directory, there were active churches of other religions in Charleston during that period. There are ministers of a majority of the religions which were known to be active in South Carolina during the latter part of the eighteenth century listed in the 1790 and 1794 city directories.

A count of the church officials is shown below.

    1782   2

    1790   13

    1794   14

Church Officials

1782

Names	Occupations	Addresses
Cooper, Rev. Robert	Rector of St. Philip's	78 Church street

Names	*Occupations*	*Addresses*
Jenkins, Rev. Edward	Rector of St. Michael's	70 Meeting street

1790

Names	*Occupations*	*Addresses*
Azabee, Abraham	rabbi	6 Beresford's street
Fabre, John Rev. C.	Rect. Luth. Ch.	31 Archdale street
Frost, Rev. Thomas	assist. St. P. Ch.	21 Archdale street
Furman, Rev. Richard	past. Bap. Ch.	19 Church street
Harris, John Hartley	c. St. Phil. Ch.	113 Queen street
Hollingshead, Rev. W^m.	past. con. ch.	93 Meeting street
Jean, Paul Costa	Jewish priest	83 Church street
Jenkins, Rev. Edward		84 Tradd street
Keith, Rev. Issac S.	past. con. ch.	76 Church street
Mills, Rev. Mr. ___	R. St. And. ch.	47 Tradd street
Nixon, Rev. William	colum. acad.	New Market
Purcell, Dr. Henry	rect. St. M. ch.	89 Tradd street
Smith, Rev. Dr. Robert	R. St. Phil. ch.	St. Philips parsonage
Smith, Rev. William		St. Philip's academy

1794

Names	*Occupations*	*Addresses*
Anderson, John	clergyman	183 King street
Buist, George rev.	P. Presb. church	28 Meeting street
Dater, Frederick rev.		25 King street
Fabre, John rev.	R. lutheran c.	31 Archdale street
Frost, Thomas rev.		20 Archdale street
Furman, Richard	pastor baptist c.	19 Church street
Gates, Thomas rev.		98 Meeting street
Hammett, William rev.	P. Trinity ch.	Maiden lane
Holinshead, William	P. independ. c.	94 Meeting street
Jenkins, Edward rev.		6 Lamboll street
Keith, Isaac S. rev.	P. Indepen. ch.	59 Queen street
M'Koy, Abraham F.	clk. St. Philips	___
Purcell, Henry, rev.	R. St. Michael	89 Tradd street
Smith, Robert, rev.	R. St. Philips	Wentworth street

Chapter VII / Medical Community

Charleston for many years had a large number of medical persons in relation to the number of inhabitants. This can be attributed to several factors. The high incidence of disease in the area, particularly yellow fever and malaria attracted members of the medical profession. The medical profession was considered a respectable profession for young gentlemen. The practice of medicine was not strictly regulated during this era. However, following the Revolutionary War, the medical profession was thinned by the banishment of thirteen doctors because of their Loyalist sympathies and activities.

Prior to 1765, when the first medical college was established in the colonies, all legitimate physicians in the New World were educated abroad, usually at Leyden or Edinburgh. Many of the physicians of Charleston took an interest in scientific investigation. A few wrote papers which were published in leading European scientific journals of the day.

Many physicians prepared their own medicines and many apothecaries practiced medicine. Since the functions of the physicians and apothecaries seem to overlap, apothecaries have been included in this section. Midwives, who took the place of a physician or obstetrician in the delivery of babies, are also included in this section.

In some instances the sole indication of the profession of doctor is the title affixed to the name. Therefore, it is possible that the list may include a doctor of divinity or doctor of laws.

A count of the medical community is shown below.

Medical Community

	1782	1790	1794
apothecary		2	6
dentist		1	1
Dr.	14		
midwife			4
physician	2	23	25

surgeon   1   4   1

Medical Community

1782

Names	Occupations	Addresses
Baron, Dr. Alexander		73 Broad street
Brown & Grant	surgeons	85 Church street
Carter, Dr. George		70 Broad street
Clitherall, Dr. James		51 Tradd street
Fyffe, Dr. Charles	Physicians to the Refugees	27 Broad street
Garden, Dr. Alexander	.	77 Broad street
Halmbaum, Dr. George		10 Moore street
Harris, Dr. Tucker		147 King street
Hayes, Dr. ___	physician to the Army	52 Tradd street
Keith, Dr. William		11 Queen street
Logan, Dr. George		18 Tradd street
Peronneau, Dr. Robert		105 Meeting street
Poinsett, Dr. Elisha		4 Broad street
Rose, Dr. Hugh		56 Church street
Skene, Dr. James		65 Tradd street
Turnbull, Dr. Andrew		80 Broad street
Wilson, Dr. Robert		96 Broad street

1790

Names	Occupations	Addresses
Barron, Alexander	physician	248 Meeting street
Budd, John	physician	45 Church street
Carnes, John	apothecary	119 Queen street
Carter, George	surgeon	111 King street
Chanler, Isaac	physician	54 Broad street
Clitheral, James	physician	44 Broad street
Fayssoux, Peter	physician	263 Meeting street
Hahnbaum, Christian	physician	235 King street
Harris, Tucker	physician	69 King street
Haunbaum, George	physician	258 King street

Names	Occupations	Addresses
Kriebel, Frederick	surgeon	15 Beresford street
Kruger, John Frederick	surgeon	198 King street
Lynah, James	physician	55 Meeting street
M'Calla, Thomas	physician	223 Meeting street
Moore, Peter Joseph	dentist	42 King street
Moses, Philip	apothecary	199 Tradd street
Moultrie, James	physician	17 South bay
Neufville, William	physician	124 Broad street
Patton, Catharine	midwife	6 East bay
Petsch, Adam	physic. & bot.	241 King street
Poinsett, Elisha	physician	5 Broad street
Poyas, John Earnest	physician	4 Orange street
Ramsey, David	physician	90 Broad street
Ramsey, Joseph	physician	80 Tradd street
Read, William	physician	11 Church street
Seiger, Charles Lewis	physician	208 Meeting street
Smith, John Press	surg. & m. mid.	68 East bay
Stevens, William	physician	11 King street
Stevens, Ramsey & Co.	apothecaries	107 Broad street
Turnbull, Andrew	physician	76 East bay
Wilson, Robert	physic. & apoth.	105 Broad street
Wilson, Samuel	physician	101 Broad street

1794

Names	Occupations	Addresses
Baron, Alexander	physician	124 Queen street
Brown, Mrs. ___	midwife	46 Tradd street
Carolan, Philip	apothecary	20 Broad street
Carter, George	physician	81 Church street
Chandler & Marshall	physicians	54 Broad street
Chouler, Joseph	apothecary	123 Broad street
Clitherall, James	physician	45 Broad street
Cummings, Janet	midwife	282 King street
Fayssoux, Peter	physician	76 Tradd street
Flagg, Henry Collins	physician	9 Cumberland street
Flagg, Samuel Hort	dentist	Church street
Graham, Mary	midwife	107 Tradd street
Harris, Tucker	physician	69 King street
Haunbaum, Christian	physician	7 Moore street
Haunbaum, George	physician	258 King street
Irvine, Matthew	physician	Bay

Names	*Occupations*	*Addresses*
Lehre, William	physician	11 Liberty street
Lynah, James	physician	55 Meeting street
M'Calla, Thomas H.	physician	10 Elliott street
Moore, Joseph Pitt	surgeon	42 King street
Moses, Philip	apothecary	119 Tradd street
Moultrie, James	physician	4 Cumberland street
Neufville, William	physician	85 Tradd street
Patton, Catharine	midwife	117 Queen street
Pestch, Adam	physician	241 King street
Pointset, Elisha	physician	5 Broad street
Poyas, John Ernest	physician	4 Orange street
Ramsay, David	physician	90 Broad street
Read, William	physician	11 Church street
Sarzedas, David	apothecary	2 Beresford street
Sheed, William	apothecary	106 King street
Stephens, William S.	physician	11 King street
Stephens & Ramsay	physicians	110 Broad street
Vansilver, ___	physician	113 King street
Wilson, Robert	apothecary	103 Broad street
Wilson, Samuel	physician	101 Broad street
Wood, Thomas	physician	84 East bay

Chapter VIII / Vendue Masters and Auctioneers

The number of vendue masters and auctioneers during the period 1782 through 1794 indicates that there were many public sales during this period.

In 1784 the City Corporation limited sales to Tuesday and Thursday and prohibited the sales from taking place in the streets. Some of the vendue masters claimed that the City Corporation prohibited the street sales because the City Corporation had rented the cellars below the Exchange to auctioneers. These irate vendue masters alleged that the lower end of Broad street was blocked by the auctioneers' customers. This issue involved the protection of individual rights and would be resolved in the nineteenth century.

A count of the vendue masters and auctioneers is shown below.

Vendue Masters and Auctioneers

	1782	1790	1794
auctioneer		16	
vendue cryer			1
vendue master	8		1

Vendue Masters and Auctioneers

1782

Names	Occupations	Addresses
Cooke & Webb	vendue masters	Broad street
Currie & Norris	vendue masters	1 Bay
Jacobs, Jacob	vendue masters	34 Bay
Morris, John	vendue master	43 Bay
Risk, Hugh & Co.	vendue master	19 Church street
Russel, William	vendue master	2 Stoll's alley
Stewart, Thomas & Co.	vendue master	42 Bay
Watson & Dennison	vendue master	3 Broad street

1790

Names	Occupations	Addresses
Cambridge, Tobias	auctioneer	7 Orange street
Campbell, Laurence	auctioneer	1 Raper's alley
Cohen, Jacob	auctioneer	South side of exchange
Colcock, Job	auctioneer	109 Tradd street
Colcock and Graham	auctioneers	N. side of Exchange
Denoon, David & Co.	auctioneer	Beale's wharf
Doggett, Henry	auctioneer *ft.*	Beale's wharf
Doggett, Henry	auctioneer *dw,*	57 Church street
Gaultier, Joseph	auctioneer	92 Tradd street
Holmes, William	auctioneer	North side the Exchange
Jacobs, Jacob	auctioneer	Under the Exchange
Jacobs, Jacob *dw.*	auctioneer	20 Meeting street
M'Comb, James	auctioneer	behind the exchange
Myers, Joseph	auctioneer	Back of the Exchange
Serjeant & Cambridge	auctioneer	Beale's wharf
Timmons, Lewis	auctioneer	11 Guignard street

1794

Names	Occupations	Addresses
Cambridge, Tobias	vendue master	7 Orange street
Campbell, Laurence	vendue master	13 Ellery street
Cohen, Isaac	vendue master	227 King street
Cohen, Jacob	vendue master	267 King street
Conyers, John	vendue master	2 Stolls alley
Denoon, David & co.	vendue master	South side exchange
Depass, Ralph	vendue master	10 Union continued
Edwards, John	auctioneer	7 Meeting street
Gaultier, Joseph	vendue cryer	92 Tradd street
Holmes, William	vendue master	314 King street
Jacobs, Jacob	vendue master	20 Meeting street
Jacobs, Jacob, junior	vendue master	35 King street
Legge, Edward	vendue master	45 Trott street
Lopez, David & Aaron	vendue master	86 Tradd street
Macomb, James	vendue master	152 Meeting street
Sergeant, William	vendue master	6 Church street
Taylor, Joseph G.	vendue master	7 Cumberland street
Timmons, Lewis	vendue master	102 Queen street

Chapter IX / Legal Community

During the pre-Revolutionary era the legal profession was considered
a suitable career for a South Carolina gentleman and it opened the door to
a political career. The young South Carolina aristocrats who went abroad
for education were educated in law in preparation for their responsibilities
as members of the ruling class. Almost all the political leaders of pre-
Revolutionary Charleston had been educated at the Inns of Court. The sons
of the South Carolina aristocracy accounted for the largest representation
of any American colony at the Inns of Court. However, only a few of these
ever pursued law as profession.

Prior to the Revolution the chief justice and his fellow judges set the
qualifications for admission to the bar. To qualify, one must have studied
five years in Carolina or three in Carolina and two abroad.

Following the Revolution changes were made in the requirements for
admissions to the bar in South Carolina. In 1784 one had to study four years
in a South Carolina law office or study sufficiently in a foreign nation
to qualify for that nation's bar. The legislature eased the requirements
in 1785 when a county court system was created. Then citizens, who had been
a resident of any state for four years, could qualify for the bar by
examination before the judges of the Court of Common Pleas. Those who served
clerkships and studied abroad were also required to pass examinations.

Before the Revolution lawyers were largely used in the securing of debts,
and those who got the business of the large London merchants earned the
largest fees. In post-Revolutionary Charleston, there was a demand for
lawyers to straighten the property entanglements left by the war and
to serve the mercantile community in the collection of debts, etc.

A count of the members of the legal community is shown below.

Legal Community

	1782	1790	1794
attorney	11	29	42
barrister		1	2
counsellor at law		3	1

Legal Community

1782

Names	Occupations	Addresses
Bay, Elihu-Hall	attorney at law	54 Broad street
Colcok, John	attorney at law	73 Church street
Glen, John	attorney at law	30 Meeting street
Hepburn, James	attorney at law	95 Church street
Johnston, James	attorney at law	2 St. Michael's Alley
Johnston, Robert	attorney at law	2 St. Michael's Alley
Phepoe, Thomas	attorney at law	74 Broad street
Print, William	attorney at law	41 Broad street
Troup, John	attorney at law	51 Tradd street
Ward, Joshua	attorney at law	11 Tradd street
Williams, Robert	attorney at law	16 Tradd street

1790

Names	Occupations	Addresses
Archibald, George	attorney at law	48 Broad street
Bay, Elihu-Hall	attorney at law	240 Meeting street
Calhoun, John Ewing	attorney at law	127 King street
Davis, L. H.	attorney at law	93 Queen street
Deas, William	attorney at law	52 Meeting street
Desaussure, H. William	attorney at law	30 Tradd street
Drayton, Jacob	attorney at law	56 Meeting street
Drayton, John	attorney at law	42 Meeting street
Edwards, Alexander	attorney at law	6 Meeting street
Ford, J.	attorney at law	30 Tradd street
Fowke, Chandler D.	attorney at law	104 Broad street
Fraser, William	attorney at law	89 Broad street
Gaillard, Theodore, jun.	attorney at law	45 Tradd street
Holmes, John B.	attorney at law	6 Meeting street
Knight, Christopher	attorney at law	225 Meeting street
Lance, Lambert	attorney at law	90 Queen street
Lee, Thomas	attorney at law	91 Broad street
M'Call, Hext	attorney at law	267 Meeting street
M'Intosh, Simon	attorney at law	30 Beaufain street
Marshall, William	attorney at law	38 Tradd street
Mitchell, Wm. Boone	attorney at law	264 Meeting street

Names	Occupations	Addresses
Parker, John, jun.	attorney at law	41 Meeting street
Parker, Thomas	attorney at law	41 Meeting street
Pinckney, Char. C.	coun. at law	92 East bay
Read, Jacob	barrister at law	131 East bay
Rutledge, Edward	coun. at law	55 Broad street
Rutledge, Hugh	coun. at law	3 Short street
Smith, James	attorney at law	30 Church street
Taylor, George	attorney at law	228 Meeting street
Troup, John	attorney at law	117 Tradd street
Ward, John	attorney at law	255 Meeting street
Ward, Joshua	attorney at law	255 Meeting street
Winstanley, Thomas	attorney at law	2 Scarborough street

1794

Names	Occupations	Addresses
Bailey, Henry	attorney	6 Meeting street
Bee, Thomas, jun.	attorney at law	100 Church street
Darrell, Edward, junior	attorney at law	42 Broad street
Dart, Isaac Motte	attorney at law	Ansonborough
Davis, Lightfoot H.	attorney at law	93 Queen street
Desaussure, Henry Wm.	attorney at law	30 Tradd street
Desaussure & Ford	attorneys at law	29 Tradd street
Dickenson, Francis	attorney at law	Cumberland street
Drayton, Jacob	attorney at law	49 Broad street
Drayton, John	attorney at law	42 Meeting street
Edwards, Alexander	attorney at law	249 Meeting street
Ford, Timothy	attorney at law	284 Meeting street
Fowke, Chandler Din.	attorney at law	51 Tradd street
Fraser, William	attorney at law	89 Broad street
Gaillard, John	attorney at law	East bay
Gaillard, Theodore	attorney at law	82 East bay
Hall, Dominick A.	attorney at law	279 King street
Harper, Robert G.	attorney at law	52 King street
Hinds, Thomas	attorney at law	30 Broad street
Johnson, William, jun.	attorney at law	___
Lance, Lambert	attorney at law	111 Friend street
Lee, Thomas	attorney at law	208 Meeting street
M'Intosh, Simon	attorney at law	16 Friend street
Marshall, William	attorney at law	43 Meeting street
Mitchell, William Boone	attorney at law	264 Meeting street
Norris, Andrew	attorney at law	120 King street

Names	Occupations	Addresses
Parker, Thomas	attorney at law	41 Meeting street
Parker, Wm. M'Kenzie	attorney at law	Meeting street
Payton, Richard Henry	attorney at law	47 Tradd street
Peace, Joseph	attorney at law	Tradd street
Pickens, Ezekiel	attorney at law	100 Meeting street
Pinckney, Charles C.	attorney at law	92 East bay
Read, Jacob	barrister at law	121 East bay
Robertson, William	attorney at law	Church & Broad streets
Rutledge, Edward	barrister at law	55 Broad street
Rutledge, Edward, jun.	attorney at law	106 Tradd street
Smith, James	attorney at law	53 Meeting street
Smith, Thomas Rhett	attorney at law	30 Church street
Taylor, George	attorney at law	227 Meeting street
Torrance, William H.	attorney at law	112 East bay
Trezevant, Lewis	attorney at law	43 Church street
Troup, John	attorney at law	117 Tradd street
Ward, John	attorney at law	Lamboll street
Ward, Joshua	counsellor	255 Meeting street
Weston, John Holybush	attorney at law	Church street
Winstanley, Thomas	attorney at law	Scarborough street

Charleston became a major seaport early in its history. It was the
center of an inland water system that stretched from the Cape Fear River
in North Carolina to the St. John's River in Florida. By the middle of the
eighteenth century these waterways had become the chief roads to market.

Vessels, such as ships, brigantines, snows, schooners, and sloops, came
to Charleston to carry the crops to market. Men from all parts of the
Atlantic world came to Charleston on these sailing vessels. Charleston was
a major commercial center from the 1730's to the 1820's. Thus, ship masters,
pilots, mariners, and seamen were a vital part of the Charleston commercial
community during this era.

A count of the ship masters, pilots, mariners, and seamen is shown below.

Ship Masters, Pilots, Mariners, and Seamen

	1782	1790	1794
branch pilot for the bar and harbour of Charleston		15	
full branch pilot for the bar and harbour of Charleston			10
mariner		44	4
pilot		8	8
seaman		2	
ship-master		1	24

Ship Masters, Pilots, Mariners, and Seamen

1790

Names	Occupations	Addresses
Akin, Thomas	mariner	97 East bay

Names	Occupations	Addresses
Anthony, Emanuel	mariner	24 Elliot street
Bass, John	mariner	10 Orange street
Boibliat, Peter	mariner	5 Price's alley
Briendly, Stephen	pilot	2 Greenwood's alley
Brown, Jeremiah	mariner	Lynch's lane
Brown, Roger	mariner	27 Pinckney street
Butterton, Joseph	branch pilot for the bar and harbour of Charleston	
Butterton, Joseph	pilot	7 Maiden lane
Cameron, Andrews	seaman	37 Pinckney street
Cap. Dominick	mariner	Lambell's lane
Coates, Thomas	mariner	97 East bay
Cozens, Matthew	mariner	3 Beresford's alley
Cuppage, Hugh	mariner	225 Meeting street
Curry, William	seaman	34 Pinckney street
Darrell, Benjamin	mariner	22 Meeting stree
Dickenson, Jeremiah	mariner	9 Cumberland street
Ditcham, John	mariner	38 Hasell street
Ears, William	branch pilot for the bar and harbour of Charleston	
Eldridge, Randall	mariner	117 East bay
Ellis, John	mariner	Wyat's lot
Farrow, William	branch pilot for the bar and harbour of Charleston	
Forrester, William	mariner	172 Meeting street
Gordon, John	pilot	22 Guignard street
Gordon, John	branch pilot for the bar and harbour of Charleston	
Hall, William	mariner	5 Cumberland street
Halliday, George	mariner	106½ East bay
Hill, Duncan	mariner	96 Church street
Hogan, David Henry	mariner	2 King street
Johnson, William	mariner	16 Friend street
Keen, Thomas	mariner	16 Union street continued
M'Kenzie, John	branch pilot for the bar and harbour of Charleston	
M'Kenzie, John	pilot	2 Charles street
Manning, Hugh	mariner	Market-square
Marston, Nathaniel	mariner	27 Pinckney street
Matthews, Peter	mariner	22 Trott street
Meckleswitz, Felix de	mariner	Magazine street
Milligan, John	mariner	Lamboll's lane

Names	Occupations	Addresses
Minott, William	mariner	Lynch's lane
Mitchell, Lazarus	mariner	20 Beresford street
Moncrieff, John	mariner	34 Guignard street
Newton, Downham	mariner	21 Society street
Prince, Charles	pilot	115 Tradd street
Prince, Charles	branch pilot for the bar and harbour of Charleston	
Quingin, David	mariner	Roper's wharf
Rainer, David	branch pilot for the bar and harbour of Charleston	
Rainer, David	pilot	8 Maiden lane
Rice, Thomas	branch pilot for the bar and harbour of Charleston	
Rice, Thomas	pilot	115 Queen street
Ripley, Paul	branch pilot for the bar and harbour of Charleston	
Ripley, Paul	pilot	23 Beresford's alley
Ross, Thomas	mariner	95 Queen street
Saults, John	mariner	11 Chalmer's alley
Secrists, Martin	mariner	11 Amen street
Seymour, Isaac	mariner	257 Meeting street
Shultz, Daniel	mariner	20 Trott street
Smith, John	mariner	42 Church street
Smith, Thomas	branch pilot for the bar and harbour of Charleston	
Smith, Thomas	mariner	18 Pinckney street
Stone, Samuel	mariner	2 Stoll's alley
Swain, Luke	mariner	3 Stoll's alley
Thompson, John	mariner	24 Tradd street
Thomson, John	ship-master	22 Church street
Torry, Elias	branch pilot for the bar and harbour of Charleston	
Torry, Elias	pilot	6 Maiden lane
Tucker, Benjamin	mariner	265 Meeting street
Turner, Shadrack	branch pilot for the bar and harbour of Charleston	
Waldren, Samuel	branch pilot for the bar and harbour of Charleston	
Webster, Thomas	branch pilot for the	

Names	*Occupations*	*Addresses*
	bar and harbour of Charleston	
Young, Gideon	branch pilot for the bar and harbour of Charleston	

1794

Names	*Occupations*	*Addresses*
Bass, John	ship-master	88 East bay
Boulliat, Peter	ship-master	10 St. Philip's street
Bouteille, Jean	ship-master	10 Queen street
Brindley, Stephen	pilot	17 Maiden lane
Brindly, Stephen	full branch pilot for the bar and harbour of Charleston	
Brown, Daniel	mariner	3 Pinckney street
Brown, Roger	mariner	27 Pinckney street
Burrows, Frederick	full branch pilot for the bar and harbour of Charleston	
Burrows, Frederick	pilot	5 Trott street
Butterton, Joseph	full branch pilot for the bar and harbour of Charleston	
Butterton, Joseph	pilot	1 Rhett street
Connelly, John	ship-master	21 Meeting street
Darrell, Benjamin	ship-master	23 Meeting street
Dickerson, Jeremiah	ship-master	10 Cumberland street
Eyers, William	pilot	8 Pinckney street
Hall, William	ship-master	5 Cumberland street
Hill, Duncan	ship-master	106 East bay
Hunt, ___	ship-master	23 Berresford street
Hunter, Thomas	ship-master	67 Church street
Keen, Thomas	ship-master	12 Union continued
M'Kenzie, John	full branch pilot for the bar and harbour of Charleston	
Milligan, John	ship-master	34 Archdale street
Minott, William	mariner	301 King street
Moore, John	ship-master	East bay
Mucklehany, James	full branch pilot for	

Names	Occupations	Addresses
	the bar and harbour of Charleston	
Newton, Downham	ship-master	Society street
Prince, Charles	full branch pilot for the bar and harbour of Charleston	
Prince, Charles	pilot	13 King street
Revell, John	ship-master	20 Guignard street
Rolander, Henry	ship-master	16 Tradd street
Ross, Thomas	ship-master	101 Queen street
Secrists, Martin	mariner	11 Amen street
Seymour, Isaac	ship-master	20 Lynch's lane
Seymour, Stephen	ship-master	116 Church street
Shanks, Joseph	mariner	35 Meeting street
Smith, Thomas	full branch pilot for the bar and harbour of Charleston	
Smith, Thomas	ship-master	20 Guignard street
Stone, Samuel	ship-master	4 Stoll's alley
Swain, Joseph	full branch pilot for the bar and harbour of Charleston	
Swain, Joseph	pilot	2 Stoll's alley
Swain, Luke	full branch pilot for the bar and harbour of Charleston	
Swain, Luke	pilot	3 Stoll's alley
Thomson, Archibald	ship-master	66 East bay
Thomson, John	ship-master	22 Church street
Tucker, Benjamin	ship-master	114 Church street
Vanassendelst, Willaim	ship-master	23 Trott street
Webster, Thomas	pilot	Wyatt's square
Young, Gideon	full branch pilot for the bar and harbour of Charleston	

Chapter XI / Civil and Military Officials

The government of South Carolina changed tremendously during the period from 1776 to 1790. These vast changes were reflected in the government of the City of Charleston.

The First Continental Congress began its sessions in Philadelphia on September 5, 1774. The members agreed to organize an economic boycott of Great Britain and to reconvene if further action proved to be necessary. Events began to move in the direction of an appeal to arms. Finally, the British commander felt obliged to seize the military supplies which the militant leaders of the colonies had accumulated at Concord. On April 19, 1775, the British troops entered Lexington and were met by a company of armed militia. A shot was fired and the Revolutionary War began. The British troops moved on to Concord and destroyed some American supplies. Farmers and militiamen lined the road and picked off the British troops on their return to Boston from Lexington and Concord.

On May 10, 1775, the Second Continental Congress met in Philadelphia. On June 15 Congress took over the command of the troops who had gathered near Boston and formed the Continental Army. The Continental Congress also assumed authority to direct the course of the war.

In March, 1776, South Carolina's Provincial Congress adopted a system of government to last until England and the American colonies settled their differences. Two years later, when the likelihood of a settlement seemed impossible, a permanent form of government was established.

In 1779 England shifted the war to the South in search of allies. On May 12, 1780, the city of Charleston and about 5,000 troops were surrendered to the British. War continued in the areas around Charleston and in the backcountry until 1781. In December, 1782, the British fleet sailed from Charleston harbor.

In a special session of the South Carolina legislature convened on July 30, 1783, the city of Charleston was incorporated. The corporation was elected by the people of Charleston. Thirteen wardens and one intendant formed the corporation and were given the power to deal with riots and other disturbances. During a disturbance the intendant was to summon wardens, constables, and other city officials and take the necessary steps to restore order.

The actions of the city wardens caused great dissension among the residents of Charleston during 1784 and 1785. The wardens had been granted little judicial power in 1783. They had asked for more power and received it in 1784. Finally, they extended their powers further themselves.

In 1785 the state was divided into counties and county courts were established. Justices of the peace were appointed by the legislature and had judicial power generally over cases not involving more than £20, jurisdiction over roads, the power to license tavern keepers, and other administrative duties.

In 1787 South Carolina sent four delegates, all Charlestonians, to the Constitutional Convention. These delegates were Charles Cotesworth Pinckney; Charles Pinckney, first cousin once removed to Charles Cotesworth Pinckney; John Rutledge, whose brother, Edward, was the brother-in-law of Charles Cotesworth Pinckney; and Pierce Butler, whose wife was a cousin to the wives of Charles Cotesworth Pinckney and Edward Rutledge.

Charleston had reached the peak of her importance. South Carolina would not ratify the Constitution without Charleston, and there would not be a United States without South Carolina. South Carolina ratified the Constitution on May 23, 1788.

In 1790 South Carolina passed a new constitution which moved the seat of government from Charleston to Columbia. This constitution accepted in full the principle of religious toleration and equality. It changed the structure of government by abolishing the Privy Council. A new constitutional convention could not be called except by a two-thirds vote of all members of the legislature, and the constitution could not be amended unless a bill for amendment was passed by a two-thirds vote of the whole membership, published three months before an election, and then passed again by two-thirds of the new legislature. It also altered the apportionment of representation in both houses of the legislature. Dual offices for the treasurer, secretary of state, and surveyor-general were established in Charleston and Columbia.

In 1790 the government of South Carolina bore little resemblance to that of South Carolina at the outbreak of the American Revolution. There had truly been a revolution in South Carolina.

Civil and Military Officials

1782

Names	Occupations	Addresses
Balfour, Lt. Col. ___ Billet Office	Commandant of Charleston	94 King street 97 Broad street

Names	Occupations	Addresses
Bisbane, James	sheriff	57 Broad street
Bull, ___	Lieutenant Governour	57 Meeting street
Clark, Francis-Rush	Commissary of Forage	3 Queen street
Cooper, ___	Town-Adjutant	55 Broad street
Deveaux, Jacob	Powder Receiver	10 Tradd street
Fraser, Charles	Town-Major	87 King street
Fraser, James	Acting Barrack-master	3 Legare street
Gray, Col. ___	Paymaster of Militia	75 Tradd street
M'Kinnon, Capt. ___	D.Q.M.G.	2 Bay
Moncrieffe, Lt. Col. ___	Chief engineer	72 Broad street
Morrison, Major ___	Commissary General	103 Church street
Newton, William	Deputy paymaster	42 Meeting street
Prevost, Major ___	D. Insp. Gen. of Prov. Forces	14 Bay
Post Office		3 Legare street
Prince, Lieut. ___	D. Commissary of Naval Prisoners	55 Bay
Roupell, George	Deputy postmaster general	45 Tradd street
Savage, Edward	Judge of the Court of Vice-Admiralty	69 Church street
Skottowe, Thomas	Secretary of the Province	16 Broad street
Spooner, George	Inspector of Refugees	43 Tradd street
Traile, Major ___	Commanding officer of Artillery	25 Church street
Winstanley, Thomas	Clerk of Police	12 Elliott street
Wray, George	Commissary of Artillery	61 Church street

1790

Names	Occupations	Addresses
Aertsen, Guiliam	City Sheriff	___
Aertsen, Guilliem, Esq.	City Sheriff	259 King street
Atmar, Ralph	mesen. h. repr.	State-house yard
Bacot, Thomas Will[m].	tax collector	103 Broad street
Balantine, James	coroner	46 Tradd street
Bee, Thomas, Esq.	District Judge	100 Church street
Beekman, Samuel	Warden No. 4	___
Bentham, James	magistrate	47 Church street
Blair, William	constable	Near the old church

Names	Occupations	Addresses
Bounetheau, John	Keeper of the Exchange and Messenger to the Council	___
Bounetheau, Peter	City Clerk, City of Charleston	___
Bounnetheau, Peter	clerk c. council	30 Trott street
Bremar, Francis	surveyor general	132 King street
Brownlee, John	Warden No. 9	___
Calvert, John	inspector	86 Church street
Clementson, Alexander	dep. city sheriff	2 Wentworth street
Cole, Richard	Warden No. 8	___
Corbet, Samuel	city marshall	5½ Meeting street
Corbet, Samuel	City Marshal	___
Corbett, Thomas	Warden No. 3	___
Cripps, John Splatt	Warden No. 7	___
Crowe, Edward	custom h. boat	10 Chalmers Alley
Dart, John Sandford	clerk H.R.	At the custom house
	notary pub	& 2 Front street (remainder of address is not legible)
Dawson, Michael	constable	12½ Pinckney street
Desaussure, William H.	Warden No. 5	___
Drayton, Stephen	com. pub. rec.	26 Meeting street
Elsinore, James	clerk of treas.	12 King street
Elsworth, Theophilus	gauger customs	73 East bay
Gibbes, William Hasell	mast. chancery	57 Meeting street
Grimke. John F.	associate judge	2 Orange street
Hall, Thomas	postmaster	32 Broad street
Ham, Richard	inspector cust.	8 Chalmer's alley
Ham, Thomas	inspector cust.	24 Beresford's alley
Harris, Tucker	Warden No. 12	___
Holmes, Isaac	lieut. governor	15 Legare street
Holmes, John B.	Recorder, City of Charleston	___
Hort, William	state treas.	28 Guignard street
Howell, John	constable	17 Beresford street
Huger, Isaac, jun.	sheriff C. D.	59 Broad street
Huger, Isaac, sen.	distr. marshall	59 Broad street
Hutson, Richard	chancellor	102 Tradd street
Kaiser, John	deputy sheriff	274 King street
Kalcoffen, John	constable	78 Church street
Kalteisen, Michael	com. f. Johnson	13 Maiden lane
Knox, Robert	cont. state meas.	17 Union street continued
Legare, Benjamin	justice peace	11 Stoll's alley
Lining, Charles	ord. & attorney	17 Friend street
Logan, George	state physician	32 Tradd street
M'Call, James	auditorgeneral	88 Church street

Names	Occupations	Addresses
M'Call, John	city treasurer	110 Church street
M'Lane, John	mast. poor h.	1 Mazyck street
Marshall, William	Warden No. 10	___
Mason, William	clerk com. pl.	49 Broad street
Mathews, John	chancellor	85 East bay
Mazyck, Daniel	dep. secretary	41 Trott street
Milligan, Jacob	intell. office	3 Champney's row
Milligan, James	goal keeper	New goal
Milligan, John	inspect. cust.	3 Lodge alley
Mitchell, John	Warden No. 2	___
Morgan, Edward	cust. h. boat	Cochran's wharf
Morris, Thomas	Warden No. 1	___
Motte, Isaac	naval officer	262 Meeting street
Moultrie, Alexander	attorney gen.	17 South bay
Muller, Albert Arney	powder rec.	Wentworth street
Neufville, John	comss. loan	85 Queen street
Neufville, John, jun.	register chan.	33 Meeting street
Palmer, John	constable	3 Water street
Peace, Isaac	Warden No. 6	___
Petry, Monsieur ___	V. C. of France	279 King street
Pilsbury, Samuel	inspect. of cust.	43 Union street
Pinckney, Charles	governor	270 Meeting street
Poyas, John E.	Warden No. 11	___
Primrose, Nicol	inspector cust.	St. Philip's street
Pringle, John Julius	U. S. Attorney	105 Tradd street
Quin, Robert	constable	12 Allen street
Reese, John	custom h. boat	31 Pinckney street
Robertson, John	Warden No. 13	___
Robertson, John	Warden No. 13	128 King street
Rutledge, John, sen.	assoc. J. U. S.	82 Broad street
Steel, William	inspect. cust.	40 Elliot street
Stevens, Cotton Mather	ward. work h.	Savage's Green
Timothy, Ann	state printer	84 Broad street
Trescot, Edward	tax collector	82 Meeting street
Vanderhorst, Arnoldus	city intendant	15 East bay
Vanderhorst, Arnoldus, Hon. Esq.	Intendant, Corporation of the City of Charleston	___
Walker, Sylvanus	tobacco insp.	2 Quince's street
Waring, Thomas	commiss. s. est.	40 Meeting street
Warley, Foelix	clerk of senate	22 Society street
Waties, Thomas	associate judge	87 East bay
Welch, John	tobacco insp.	5 Union street
Weyman, Edward	surveyor cust.	50 Churh (*sic*) street
Wood, William	inspect. cust.	22 Archdale street
Yates, William	constable	35 Union street

1794

Names	Occupations	Addresses
Aertson, Guiliam	City Sheriff	___
Aertson, Guilliam	city sheriff	15 Friend street
Alexander, Abraham	clk. in S. treas^y	24 Berresford street
Atmar, Ralph, sen.	messenger H. R.	back state house
Bay, Elihu Hall	associate judge	239 Meeting street
Beard, Jonas	powder receiver	Magazine street
Bee, Thomas, sen.	F. district judge	100 Church street
Bentham, James	justice of the peace	47 Church street
Black, Nathaniel	inspect. customs	7 Ellery street
Bonetheau, John	Keeper of the Exchange, and Messenger to the Council	
Bonetheau, Peter	city clerk	30 Trott street
Bonetheau, Peter	City Clerk, City of Charleston	___
Bremar, Francis	surveyor general	23 Trott street
Burke, AEdanus	associate judge	138 Church street
Byrne, Patrick	clk. to supervisor	129 Queen street
Carradeaux, General ___		Wentworth stret
Christie, Edward	inspect. customs	8 Chambers' alley
Clarke, Jeremiah	clerk of markets	15 Chambers' alley
Cochran, Robert	com. rev. cutter	74 Meeting street
Corbet, Samuel	City Marshal, City of Charleston	___
Corbett, Samuel	city marshall	___
Corbett, Samuel	city marshall	232 Meeting street
Cozins, Mathew	inspect. customs	5 Lodge alley
Crowe, Edward	custom h. boat	Pinckney street
Cunnington, William	justice of peace	N. of exchange
Dart, John Sandford	notary pub.	2 Front
	clerk H. R.	Ansonborough
Elsworth, Theophilus	guager for cust.	135 Queen street
Flemming, John	city-guard	44 King street
Fonspertuis, citizen ___	French consul	127 King street
Fraser, John	inspect. customs	9 Bedon's alley
Freneau, Peter	sec. of the state	Society street
Gadsden, Philip	Warden No. 4	___
Geddis, Henry	Warden No. 12	___
Gervais, John Lewis	com'r. P. acc'ts.	70 Broad street
Gibbes, William Hasell	master in chan.	57 Meeting street
Grant, Hary	agent to C. M.	East bay
Grimke, John F.	associate judge	29 Church street
Hall, Dominick A.	Warden No. 11	___

Names	Occupations	Addresses
Hall, Thomas	Warden No. 6	___
Hall, Thomas	clerk F. court	32 Broad street
Hall, Walter	justice of peace	14 King street
Handy, Thomas	constable	6 Berresford's alley
Hayes, James	constable	Union continued
Holmes, Isaac	coll. of customs	16 Legare street
Holmes, John B.	Intendant, City of Charleston	___
Holmes, John Bee	intendant	6 Meeting street
Hort, William	state treasurer	East bay
Huger, Daniel Lionel	federal marshal	Broad street
Izard, Ralph, senior	senator to U. S.	
Kaltiesen, Michael	C. fort Johnson	Maiden lane
Ladson, James	lieut. governor	14 Meeting street
Lehre, Thomas	Warden No. 10	
Linning, Charles	ordinary	10 Legare street
M'Call, John	City Treasurer, City of Charleston	___
M'Call, John	city treasurer	110 Church street
M'Carty, William	constable	22 Berresford street
M'Khugo, Anthony	inspect. customs	63 Meeting street
Marshall, William	Recorder of City of Charleston	___
Martin, John C.	Warden No. 8	___
Mason, William	clk. C.C.P.	52 Broad street
Mathews, John	chancellor	85 East bay
Mazyck, Daniel	regist. mesne C.	1 West street
Milligan, Jacob	Harbour Master	___
Milligan, Jacob	harbour master	N. E. of exchange
Milligan, James	goaler	Goal
Mitchell, John	notary public	30 East bay
Moodie, Benjamin	British consul	120 Broad street
Moore, John	lieut. R. cutter	3 Unity alley
Motte, Isaac	naval officer	262 Meeting street
Moultrie, Alexander	advocate	4 Cumberland street
Moultrie, William	governor	60 Meeting street
Neufville, John, jun.	R. court equity	32 Meeting street
Osborne, Thomas	sheriff C. T. D.	Lamboll street
Pelsberry, Samuel	inspect. customs	20 Guignard street
Primrose, Nichol	inspect. customs	St. Philips street
Pringle, John Julius	state attorney	105 Tradd street
Purcell, Joseph	Warden No. 13	___
Ramsey, David	Warden No. 7	___
Roper, Thomas	Warden No. 3	___
Rutledge, Hugh	chancellor	14 Short street
Rutledge, John	chief justice	82 Broad street
Shand, Robert	inspect. customs	5 Union street

Names	Occupations	Addresses
Simons, Keating	Warden No. 1	___
Singleton, Thomas	tobac. inspector	175 King street
Smith, Morton	insp. ct. customs	78 Church street
Stevens, Daniel	supervisor	41 George street
Stevens, Jarvis Henry	deputy sheriff	256 Meeting street
Theus, James	Warden No. 2	___
Timothy & Mason	state printers	44 East bay
Trescot, Edward	tax receiver	83 Meeting street
Turner, David Watson	deputy sheriff	Quince street
Wallis, James	custom H. boat	Champney's row
Warley, Felix	clk. the senate	44 Trott street
Waties, Thomas	associate judge	20 Legare street
Welch, John	tobac. inspector	Boundary street
Weyman, Edward	surveryor cust.	8 Chambers' alley
Wood, William	inspect. customs	5 Hopkins lane
Wrainch, John	clk. to commis.	King street

Chapter XII / Other Residents: 1782, 1790, and 1794

This chapter includes those residents who are listed in the city directories of 1782, 1790, and 1794 for whom there is no occupation listed or whose occupations are not included in the occupational categories discussed in the preceding chapters.

A count of the various categories of residents is shown below.

Other Residents

	1782	1790	1794
banker	1		
botantist		2	
cashier (bank)			1
clerk		9	4
clerk (bank)			4
colsbaun keep.		1	
comedian			1
com. loan officer		1	
com. of loans			1
C. P. accounts			1
express rider			1
lamp lighter			1
land surveyor		1	
librarian		1	1
marine hospital		1	1

money collector		1	1
money dunner			1
musician		1	
notary public		1	
organist		1	
other (no occupation listed)	18	190	184
overseer		1	
president (bank)			1
runner (bank)			1
scrivener		8	12
seedsman		1	
shrub w. house			1
surveyor			5
teller (bank)			1
violin player		1	
waiter (bank)			1

Other Residents

1782

Names	Occupations	Addresses
Biddulph, Robert	banker	9 Legare street
Bull, William, jun., Esq.		67 Tradd street
Dawson, Mrs. Christian		92 Meeting street
Deas, John, Esq.		67 Meeting street
Downes, Arthur		48 Tradd street
Gordon, Thomas-Knox (Hon.)		1 Short street
Harleston, John, Esq.		68 Tradd street
Hooper, Thomas & Co.		91 Broad street

Names	Occupations	Addresses
Hopton, William, Esq.		116 Meeting street
Lowndes, Rawlins, Esq.		63 Broad street
Mazyck, Isaac, Esq.		86 Broad street
Mazyck, Stephen, Esq.		85 Broad street
Peronneau, Henry, Esq.		105 Meeting street
Philp, Robert, Esq.		25 Queen street
Pinckney, Charles, Esq.		2 Orange street
Roper, William		52 Bay
Rose, John, Esq.		8 Bay continued
Wragg, John, Esq.		55 Broad street
Wright, Alexander, Esq.		40 Meeting street

1790

Names	Occupations	Addresses
Abrahams, Emanuel	scrivener	256 King street
Abrahams, Judah		94 Tradd street
Adamson, Jane		28 Queen street
Alexander, Abraham	scrivener	224 King street
Anderson, Ann		19 Union street continued
Andrews, Jane		243 Meeting street
Arnst, Mary		61 Queen street
Arnts, Margaret		15 Dutch church alley
Ashton, Sarah		5 Maiden lane
Audley, Martha		23 King street
Axton, Elizabeth		127 Church street
Ball, Ann		17 Church street
Ball, Elizabeth		15 Church street
Bampfield, Rebecca		39 Church street
Barnett, Ann		2 St. Michael's alley
Bayley, William, Esq.		East bay
Beale, John, Esq.		34 East bay
Bee, Mary		6 Wragg's alley
Bellamy, Hester		33 King street
Berwick, Ann		16 South bay
Bird, Elizabeth		13 Union street continued
Boderum, Joseph	clerk	7 Pinckney street
Bogie, Agnes		184 King street
Bolton, Martha		1 Pinckney street
Booner, Dolly		106 King street
Boucheneau, Charles	scrivener	170 Meeting street
Bowing, George		13 Moore street

Names	*Occupations*	*Addresses*
Brady, Mary		82 Church street
Brailsford, Samuel		1 Friend street
Brandford, Elizabeth		34 Meeting street
Brook, Mary		14 Dutch church alley
Brower, Jeremiah		13 King street
Brown, James		131 King street
Burnham, Sarah		14 Maiden lane
Cahill, Daniel	clerk	35 King street
Cain, Grace		57 Queen street
Campbell, John		Beale's wharf
Carnes, Susannah		83 Tradd street
Carson, Elizabeth		8 Wragg's alley
Cart, John, jun.	clerk	George street
Cart, John, sen.		125 Queen street
Chalmers, Elizabeth		108 Queen street
Chalmers, Rebecca		40 Trott street
Chitty, Ann		3 Moore street
Clark, John	scrivener	247 Meeting street
Clifford, Elizabeth		33 Wentworth street
Clime, Mary		138 King street
Cochran, Robert		75 Meeting street
Cogdale, Jane		180 King street
Coile, Margaret		16 Pinckney street
Collins, Mary		Wyatt's lot
Collis, Elizabeth		99 Tradd street
Cooper, James		25 Union street
Coram, Francis	scrivener	255 King street
Cowan, John	overseer	35 Pinckney street
Cox, Henrietta Maria		42 Trott street
Cox, John		3 Elliot street
Creitner, Barbara		23 Archdale street
Cromwell, Elizabeth		34 Tradd street
Cross, Susannah		10 Union street
Cudworth, Nathaniel	clerk	15 Hasell street
Cumin, Casper	violin-player	224 King street
Custer, James	clerk	26 Queen street
Custom house & naval office		7 Champney's w.
Dacosta, Sarah		25 Archdale street
Daniel, Elizabeth		2 Scarborough street
Davie, William	money collector	5 Short street
Dawes, Margaret		131 Church street
Denton, James		Fishmarket wharf
Dewar, Robert		93 Tradd street
Dewees, Sarah		10 Liberty street
Disher, Mary		1 Wragg's alley
Doughty, Abraham		9 Dutch church alley
Douxsaint, Mary Ester		84 Church street

Names	Occupations	Addresses
Drayton, Rebecca		Common street
Duval, Catharine		113 Church street
Easton, Susannah		Barracks
Edwards, John		7 Meeting street
Elliott, Elizabeth		306 King street
Emmet, Charlotte		7 Bedon's alley
Farquahar, John	scrivener	2 Pitt street
Ferguson, Ann		67 Tradd street
Fletcher, Phoebe		5 Beresford alley
Florine, Lucas		34 Guignard street
Ford, Mary		294 (illegible)
Freer, Ann		109 Church street
Freer, Sarah		31 Wentworth street
Freer, Thomas		Price's alley
Garner, Ann		Orange street
Gensill, John	marine hosp.	167 King stret
Gibbs, Amariatha		30 Queen street
Gibbs, Mary		59 Queen street
Glover, Ann		312 King street
Gordon, Mary		8 Ellery street
Gottier, Isabella		14 Mazyk (*sic*) street
Graeme, Ann		82 Queen street
Graham, Mary		108 Tradd street
Grimke, John Paul		54 Meeting street
Guerard, Mary Ann		130 Church street
Haig, Mary		10 Ellery street
Hall, Mary Ann		16 King street
Hancock, Elizabeth		6 Maiden lane
Harden, Sarah		27 Society street
Harleston, Ann		20 Hasell street
Hartley, Elizabeth		9 Meeting street
Harvey, Elizabeth		Market square
Harvey, Elizabeth		10 Dutch church alley
Hayward, Hannah		18 Church street
Hesseling, I. H.	colsbaun keep.	137 King street
Hill, Eleanor		14 Union street
Hill, Joseph		Jervey's wharf
Hope, Mary		South bay
Hopton, Sarah		81 Meeting street
House, Samuel	clerk	7 Chambers alley
Huger, John	com. loan office	73 Broad stree
Hutton, James	clerk	South bay
Irving, Beaufain John		10 Legare street
Izard, Charlotte		1 Cumberland street
Jeffries, Mary		65 Queen street
Johnston, Eliza		3 Charles street
Johnston, Hester		1 Clifford's alley

Names	*Occupations*	*Addresses*
Johnston, John	clerk	Near the old church
Jones, William	clerk	Jervey's wharf
Juhan, Alexander	musician	111 Tradd street
Kelder, Henry		7 Clifford street
Ladson, Jane		49 Tradd street
Ladson, Sarah		28½ Broad street
Lance, Ann		10 Allen street
Lane, Alice		7 King street
Lang, Jane		73 Church street
Langford, Ann		23 Guignard street
Lehre, Mary		11 Liberty street
Lennox, William		5 Orange street
Lesesne, Sarah		108 East bay
Linguard, Mary		72 Church street
Livingston, William		George street
Long, Elizabeth		178 King street
Lopez, Aaron	scrivener	2 Clifford street
Lord, Ann		25 Beaufain street
Mackie, Ann		6 Legare street
Magood, Simon		Cochran's wharf
Mapey, Catharine		261 Meeting street
Marr, Ann		132 Church street
Marrow, Elizabeth		5 Charles street
Matthews, Edith		State-house square
Mazyck, William		83 Queen street
Middleton, Mary	widow	Front street Ansonborough
Miller, Ann		15 King street
Miller, Rence		275 Meeting street
Mitchell, Elizabeth		7 Trott street
Mitchell, John	notary public	30 East bay
Mitchell, Mary		5 Moore street
Morgan, Ann		39 King street
Morris, Mary		30 Wentworth street
Morrower, Margaret		12 Pinckney street
Moses, Barnet		7 Moore street
Motter, Isaac		104 King street
Muncreef, Susannah		21 Queen street
Myers, Israel		20 Union street continued
North, Susannah		37 Tradd street
Nott, Isabella		58 Church street
Oats, Charles		26 Trott street
Oats, Edward		1 Charles street
Oliphant, Catharine		6 Union street continued
Parsons, Susannah		20 Church street
Petrie, Elizabeth		1 Orange street
Petsch, Adam	physic. & botan.	241 King street
Pinckney, Frances		270 Meeting street

Names	Occupations	Addresses
Pinckney, Frances S.		16 Legare street
Pitts, Frances		1 South bay
Powell, Ruth		2 Lynch's lane
Poyas, Magdalene		36 Meeting street
Price, Ann		52 Broad street
Prince, Ann		98 Queen street
Prioleau, Philip	librarian l. soc.	21 East bay
Pritchard, Mrs. John		4 Magazine street
Purcell, Joseph	land surveyor	121 King street
Purchess, Samuel	seedsman	39 Elliot street
Radcliffe, Elizabeth		11 George street
Ravenel, Elizabeth		107 Queen street
Rivers, Beulah	widow	7 Stoll's alley
Roberts, Ann		16 Church street
Rodamond, Rachel		Market's square
Rose, Rebecca		5 Smith's lane
Rowand, Robert		2 Friend street
Russell, Ann		Lynch's lane
St. John, Mary		11 Allen street
Sarrazin, Jonathan		9 George street
Savage, Martha		Savage's green
Savage, Mary		59 King street
Shaw, Mary Elizabeth		33 Tradd street
Shepherd, Jane		37 Meeting street
Shrewsbury, Mary		32 Pinckney street
Simons, Sampson		6 Price's alley
Singleton, Thomas		168 King street
Skirving, Charlotte		8 Church street
Smith, Daniel	scrivener	14 Society street
Smyser, Hannah		56 Church street
Smyth, John		11 Ellery street
Sommers, Martha		1 East bay
Stevens, Jervis Henry	organist	256 Meeting street
Stewart, Mary		39 Hasell street
Stock, Margaret		14 King street
Stoll, Sarah		8 Dutch church alley
Stone, Love		304 King street
Stupitch, Dr. ___	botanist	16 Beresford street
Swadler, Mary		13 Mazyck street
Sykes, Thomas		125 King street
Taggart, Mary		21 Meeting street
Tennent, Susannah		81 Tradd street
Thomas, Mary Lamboll		8 King street
Vardell, Elizabeth		19 King street
Veree, Mary		13 Church street
Wagner, George		85 Broad street
Ward, Love		315 King street

Names	*Occupations*	*Addresses*
Webb, William		14 Moore street
White, Sims		12 Ellery street
Williams, Elizabeth		17 Legare street
Williams, Isham		132 East bay
Williams, Margaret		60 Queen street
Willingham, Mary		27½ Beaufain street
Wilson, Mrs. John		51 Tradd street
Wragg, Henrietta		86 East bay

1794

Names	*Occupations*	*Addresses*
Abrahams, Emanuel	scrivener	112 King street
Adams, Samuel	surveyor	236 King street
Addison, Joseph		18 Hasell street
Anderson, Ann		14 Union continued
Ashton, Catherine		5 Maiden lane
Audley, Martha		23 King street
Bacot, Mrs. ___		103 Broad street
Bacot, Thomas Wright	cashier S. C. B.	13 Broad street
Baker, Ann		10 Church street
Ball, Ann		17 Church street
Ball, Elizabeth		18 Church street
Bampfield, George		93 Meeting street
Beale, John		34 East bay
Beekman, Bernard	surveyor	109 East bay
Bee, Elizabeth		8 Trott street
Blackie, Elizabeth		14 Church street
Blair, James	clerk B. bank	1 Stoll's alley
Blamyer, William	librarian S. C. L. S.	77 Church street
Bollough, Mary		Pinckney street
Bouchonneau, Charles	waiter B. Bank	170 Meeting street
Boyd, Elizabeth		43 Trott street
Branford, Elizabeth		34 Meeting street
Broughton, Ann		103 Tradd street
Brower, Jeremiah	scrivener	22 Berresford street
Brown, Joseph		66 Tradd street
Brown, Mary		38 Archdale street
Buckle, Thomas	scrivener	56 Broad street
Burckhart, John	express rider	13 Chalmers alley
Cam, ___	widow	127 Queen street

Names	Occupations	Addresses
Cart, Sarah		125 Queen street
Cartwright, Paul		9 Lynch's lane
Chalmers, Eliza		108 Queen street
Christian, Elizabeth		14 Trott street
Clarke, Mary		180 Meeting street
Cobia, Elizabeth		14 Berresford street
Cobia, Margaret		18 Berresford street
Coiles, Margaret		16 Pinckney street
Collins, Mary		11 Hasell street
Cook, Florence		16 Bedon's alley
Cromwell, Elizabeth		34 Tradd street
Cross, James	surveyor	11 Guignard street
Cudworth, Nathaniel	scrivener	225 Meeting street
Custer, James	scrivener	25 Queen street
Cyples, Margaret		7 Trott street
Daniel, Elizabeth		63 George street
Dart, Mrs. ___		28 Tradd street
Davie, William	money collector	9 Friend street
Deas, Elizabeth		55 Church street
Delavergene, ___		12 Moore street
Delyon, Isaac		61 King street
Depeyster, ___		7 Hasell street
Devona, ___		Wentworth street
Disher, Mary		117 East bay
Donaldson, Mary		22 Tradd street
Downey, Mrs. ___		Good bye alley
D'Oyley, Ann		82 Queen street
Drummond, Ann		22 Guignard street
Dubald, Frederick		243 King street
Durang, ___		3 Cumming street
Dursse, John		178 King street
Duvall, Catherine		113 Church street
Ehny, Catharine		14 Magazine street
Fereaud, Alexander		220 Meeting street
Ferguson, Mrs. ___		Liberty street
Florin, Lucas	clerk	34 Guignard street
Forbes, Elizabeth		104 East bay
Forrest, Michael		96 Queen street
Foster, Thomas	runner b. bank	50 Church street
Fraser, ___	widow	22 King street
Freer, Ann		109 Church street
Gadsden, Mrs. Thomas		6 Front Ansonb.
Gare, Rebecca		9 Allen street
Gaultier, Isabella		15 Mazyck street
Gensell, John	marine hospital	167 King street
Gibbes, Mary		Gibbes street
Gist, Mrs. ___ (widow of Gen. Gist)		1 Wentworth street

Names	*Occupations*	*Addresses*
Glover, Ann		312 King street
Goddard & Sturges	surveyor	93 Meeting street
Gomez, Elias		10 Allen street
Gordon, Thomas	clk. S. C. society	12 East bay
Graham, William	clerk B. Bank	35 Tradd street
Gratten, Daniel		19 Berresford street
Grimbal, Mary M.		9 Church street
Grimke, Mary		54 Meeting street
Grossman, Francis		64 Queen street
Gruber, Charles, junior		253 King street
Guerard, Mary Ann		137 Church street
Gury, Charles F.		7 Burns' lane
Haig, Mrs. ___		21 Hasell street
Hair, Edward		106 King street
Hall, Mary Ann		15 Magazine street
Hammett, Charlotte		7 Bedon's alley
Harleston, Elizabeth		20 Hasell street
Harleston, Mrs. John		106 Tradd street
Harrison, Isaac		205 Meeting street
Harvey, Elizabeth		11 Allen street
Hatter. Elizabeth		38 Queen street
Heyward, Hannah		12 Legare street
Hill, Charles	scrivener	14 Chalmers alley
Horsey, Thomas	scrivener	6 Charles street
Houlton, James	money dunner	3 Water street
Howard, Ann		183 Meeting street
Humphreys, Benjamin		9 Orange street
Hunt, Mrs. ___		Elliott street
Ingles, Alexander		12 Short street
Izard, Charlotte		3 Cumberland street
Jervey, Thomas		16 King street
Johnson, Elizabeth		3 Charles street
Johnston, Hester		1 Clifford's alley
Johnston, John	clerk	3 Ellery street
Jones, Thomas	presid't S. C. B.	4 Guignard street
Kelsall, John		306 King street
Kelsey, John		12 Trott street
Kemmell, Mrs. ___		46 Queen street
Lafaver, Miss ___		66 Meeting street
Lahogue, Feret		309 King street
Lance, Ann		12 Friend street
Langford, Ann		171 Meeting street
Legare, Elizabeth		Society street
Legare, Frances		Anson street
Lesesne, Mrs. ___		1 Hasell street
Lesesne, Mrs. ___		108 East bay
Liedenhall, Johannas		2 Gillon street

Names	Occupations	Addresses
Linguard, Mary		74 Church street
Livingston, Eleanor		62 George street
Lockwood, Joshua		1 Smith's lane
Logan, Mrs. George		32 Tradd street
Loocock, Mrs. Aaron		31 Tradd street
Lord, Mrs. Andrew		25 Beaufain street
Lord, Richard	clk. S. C. bank	43 Church street
Mann, Margaret		56 George street
Marshall, Mrs. ___		32 Guignard street
Mart, Ann		139 Church street
Martin, Daniel	lamp lighter	269 King street
Martin, Hawkins		21 King street
Mathews, Edeth		State-house square
Mazyck, Mary		101 Broad street
Middleton, Arthur		Front Ansonborough
Millin, John		13 Beresford street
Miott, Mrs. ___		126 Queen street
Mitchell, James		19 Pinckney street
Morris, Mrs. George		21 Archdale street
Mouat, Mrs. John		15 King street
Muller, Magdalen		Wentworth street
Mulligan, Francis	shrub w. house	98 East bay
Muncrieff, Mary		20 Queen street
Myers, Mary		State-house square
Nelson, James		34 Beaufain street
Neufville, John, sen.	com. of loans	85 Queen street
Niel, Rebecca		90 Queen street
North, Susannah		37 Tradd street
Parker, Samuel		110 Queen street
Parker, Sarah		11 Legare street
Parsons, Susannah		20 Church street
Pearce, Mrs. Robert		19 Hasell street
Peronneau, Mary		102 Tradd street
Petrie, Elizabeth		1 Orange street
Pinckney, Frances S.		17 Legare street
Post office		99 Church street
Postell, Susannah		4 Hopton's alley
Poyas, Magdalen		36 Meeting street
Prince, Ann		114 Queen street
Prioleau, Edith		21 Guignard street
Purcell, Joseph	surveyor	1 Liberty street
Quince, Susannah		36 Hasell street
Ransier, ___		9 Hasell street
Ratcliffe, Elizabeth		9 George street
Ravenel, Elizabeth Jane		57 George street
Ravenel, Stephen		43 Church street
Reid, George	teller S. C. bank	24 Meeting street

Names	Occupations	Addresses
Roach, William	clerk B. bank	Quince street
Roberts, Ann		16 Church street
Roper, Hannah		4 East bay
Ross, Alexander	scrivener	14 Church street
Roupell, George		18 Tradd street
Russell, Mary		1 Lynch's lane
Saylor, Elizabeth		38 Elliott street
Scotton, Susanna		179 King street
Scrivener, James	clerk	130 King street
Sheriff's Office		2 Smith's lane
Shrewsberry, Rebecca		East bay
Simons, Samuel		6 Price's alley
Skirving, Charlotte		8 Church street
Skrine, William	scrivener	303 King street
Smiser, Hannah		56 Church street
Smith, Mrs. ___		83 Queen street
Smith, Daniel	scrivener	12 Guignard street
Smith, Josiah	cashier of B. bank	2 Meeting street
Smith, Richard		18 Hasell street
Smith, Samuel	teller B. bank	98 Church street
Smith, Mrs. Thomas		19 Friend street
Spiddle, Elizabeth		6 Allen street
Stevens, Cotten Mather		256 King street
Stewart, Alexander		29 King street
Stoll, Sarah		8 Allen street
Stone, Barbary		141 Meeting street
Stone, Charles		294 King street
Stone, Isabella		35 Trott street
Stone, Love		11 Orange street
Swadler, Mary		13 Magazine street
Taggart, Mary		21 Meeting street
Tennant, Susannah		82 Tradd street
Tew, Charles	scrivener	15 Lynch's lane
Theus, Rosanna		87 Church street
Theus, Simon	C. P. accounts	271 Meeting street
Thomas, Mary Lamboll		8 King street
Tydeman, Mrs. ___		84 Queen street
Vardell, Elizabeth		19 King street
Veree, Joseph	scrivener	13 Church street
Vesier, M.		16 Beresford street
Villepontoux, Jane		5 East bay
Villeret, Mary		13 Allen street
Ward, Love		12 Church street
Waring, Mary		69 Meeting street
Warley, Elizabeth		30 Beaufain street
Wells, Richard		Pinckney street
Wesner, Philip	public house	261 King street

Names	*Occupations*	*Addresses*
West, Thomas Wade	comedian	78 Tradd street
Whitley, Moses		35 Guignard street
Williams, Elizabeth		13 Legare street
Williams, Margaret		60 Queen street
Wilson, Sarah		4 Church street
Withers, Rebecca		8 Cumberland street
Young, Sarah		81 Tradd street
Young, Susannah		257 Meeting street

The directory of residents which is commonly called the "1785 City Directory" was issued in 1784 as a part of *The South Carolina and Georgia Almanack for 1785* by John Tobler.

This directory contains the occupation of only two persons. The author has supplied some additional information concerning a few individuals from publications relating to particular trades or professions.

Names	*Occupations*	*Addresses*
Aitken, John		7 Elliott street
Alexander, Alexander		25 Union street continued
Atkinson, Joseph		103 Church street
Audley, Erasmus		5 Elliott street
Austen & Moore		24 Bay
Ball, Joseph		66 Church street
Ball, Jennings & Co.		52 Bay
Ballantine and Warham		7 Tradd street
Beard, Charles		3 Broad street
Bee, Thomas		25 Church street
Bethune, Alexander		113 Broad street
Blacklock & Tunno		26½ Broad street
Blakely, Samuel		25 Broad street
Bleakly, Archibald		Church street
Boomer, John		90 Church street
Bounetheau, Peter		1 George street
Bourdeaux, Daniel & Co.		48 Bay
Bowen & Markland		15 Meeting street
Bower, Katharine		28 Broad street
Brailsford, William		49 Bay
Brown, Jeremiah		68 Church street
Buckle, Thomas		54 Broad street
Budd, Dr. John		43 Queen street
Burd & Boden		28 Amen corner
Burgwin, Hooper & Alexander		8 Bedon's alley
Buyck, Augustinus		2 Queen street
Calvert, John		9 Church street
Cam, William		28 Bay
Campbell, Laurence		Scott's wharf
Cannon, Daniel		5 Queen street

Names	Occupations	Addresses
Cantor and Company		16 Meeting street
Cart, John & Co.		24 King street
Chandler, Dr. Isaac		52 Broad street
Childs, Nathan & Co.		85 Church street
Chisolm, Alexander & Co.		11 Elliott street
Cobham, George		20 Broad street
Cochran, Robert		25 Bay
Cohen & Alexander		At the Exchange
Colcock & Gibbons		Jervey & Walter's wharf
Conyers, Holmes & Co.		51 Bay
Cooth, James		1 Queen street
Coram, Thomas		28 Queen street
Crafts, William & Co.		5 Bay
Cripps, John Splatt & Co.		94 Broad street
Cudworth, Benjamin		2 Cumberland street
Cudworth & Waller		92 Broad street
Cunnington, William		7 Bedon's alley
Dawes, Ralph		2 Elliott street
Dillon & Chisselle		50 Queen street
Doughty, Thomas		108 Meeting street
Doughty, William		Meeting street
Drayton & Stevens		2 St. Michael's alley
DuPre, Cornelius		23 Church street
Edwards, James		Tradd street
Ellison and Dupont		3 Bedon's alley
Ellsinore, James		30½ King street
Eveleigh, Thomas & Co.		48 Bay
Farr, Thomas		87 Broad street
Ferguson, Charles		80 Tradd street
Fisher, Hughes & Edwards		6 Tradd street
Flagg, George		23 King street
Flagg, Dr. Henry-Colins		63 Tradd street
Folker, John-Casper		22 Broad street
Gaillard, Theodore		9 Bay

[N.B. Theodore Gaillard is listed as an attorney in Charleston in
1788 in John Belton O'Neall, *Biographical Sketches of the Bench and
Bar of South Carolina* (Charleston: S. G. Courtenay & Co., 1859),
Vol. II, p. 601.]

Names	Occupations	Addresses
Gibbes, William-Hasell		74 Broad street
Gibbons, John		48 Bay
Gibbs, John-Walters		11 Queen street
Gibson, Robert, jun.		50 Broad street
Gillon, Alexander		14 Bay
Gowdey, William	jeweller and gold-smith	106 Broad street

[E. Milby Burton, *South Carolina Silversmiths, 1690-1860* (Charleston:
The Charleston Museum, 1969), pp. 70-71.]

Names	Occupations	Addresses
Graaf, Sibells, Brassselman & Co.		__
Grant & Simons		41 Bay
Gratton, Francis		22 Meeting street
Gregorie, James		corner Bedon's alley and Tradd street
Grimke, John-Faucheraud		100 Meeting street

[N.B. John F. Grimke is listed as a law judge in 1779 in John Belton O'Neall, *Biographical Sketches of the Bench and Bar of South Carolina* (Charleston: S. G. Courtenay & Co., 1859, Vol. II, p. 597.]

Grimke, John-Paul	jeweller	101 Meeting street

[E. Milby Burton, *South Carolina Silversmiths, 1690-1860* (Charleston: The Charleston Museum, 1969), p. 78.]

Guerard, His Excellency Benja.		59 Queen street
Hahnbaum, Dr. George		52 King street
Hall, Thomas		30 Broad street
Hall, Daniel & Co.		5 Tradd street
Hane and Berk		100 Broad street
Harbison, John		20 Bay
Harris, Dr. Tucker		King street
Harris and Blachford		27 Tradd street
Harth, John		46 Broad street
Hatfield, John		18 Bay
Hazlehurst, Robert & Co.		44 Bay
Hort & Warley		39 Bay
Houckgeest, A. E. Van Braam		42 Bay
Hutson, Richard	Judge of Court of Equity	59 Tradd street

[John Belton O'Neall, *Biographical Sketches of the Bench and Bar of South Carolina* (Charleston: S. G. Courtenay & Co.), 1859, Vol. II, p. 597.]

Huxham, Courtney and Eales		80 Church street
Jacks, James	silversmith, goldsmith, and jeweller	Broad street

[E. Milby Burton, *South Carolina Silversmiths, 1690-1860* (Charleston: The Charleston Museum, 1968), pp. 91-96.]

Jervey and Waltes		On their Wharf
Jones, Joseph		Tradd street
Lamb, David		90 Church street
Lathrop & Snowden		29 Queen street
Lawson & Price		29 Broad street
Legare, Samuel		26 Church street
Lesterjette & Cochran		25 Bay
Ley, Francis		6 Tradd street
Lindsay, Robert and William		46 Bay
Lockey, Bradford and Co.		19½ Bay
M'Callum & Ewing		Tradd street
M'Caulay & Davis		8 Church street

Names	Occupations	Addresses
M'Clure, Cochran and Wiliam		40 Bay
M'Credie & Hamilton		11 Broad street
M'Leod, Angus		8 Tradd street
M'Leod, William & Co.		6 Elliott street
M'Whann, William		5½ Elliott street
Manson, John & Thomas		87 Church street
Mathews, Benjamin and George		26½ Church street
Mauger, John		9 Bedon's alley
Merrick & Conrse		7 Bedon's alley
Mey, Florian-Charles		18 Pinckney street
Midwood, Samuel		5¼ Elliott street
Miller, James		21 Bay
Miller, John	printer	91 Church street
Mitchell & Donnom		23 Bay
Morgan, Charles		12½ Broad street
Morris, Thomas		50 Bay
Nelson, George & Co.		19 Church street
Newhouse, Lewis & Co.		13 Queen street
Norris, Robert & Co.		5 Bedon's alley
North & Blake		43 Bay
O'Hara, Stewart & Co.		11 Elliott street
O'Hear, Theus & Legare		Eveleigh's wharf
Parker, John & William		27 Church street
Peace, Isaac & Co.		7 Elliott street
Penman, James & Edward		15 Bay
Pleym, Andrew		38 Bay
Porter, John		27 Queen street
Primerose, Thomson & Co.		Jervey & Walter's wharf
Prioleau, Samuel, jun. & Co.		Corner Broad str. &
Bay Rhodes, John		3 Tradd street
Roach, William		9 Broad street
Roberts, Thomas	bookseller	84 Church street
Russell, Jenkins & Co.		Bay
Russell, Commander Thomas		37 King street
Rutledge, Edward		53 Broad street
Rutledge, Hugh	Judge of Court of Equity	3 Queen street

[John Belton O'Neall, *Biograhical Sketches of the Bench and Bar of South Carolina* (Charleston: S. G. Courtenay & Co., 1859), Vol. II, p. 597.]

Rutledge, John	Judge of Court of Equity	72 Broad street

[John Belton O'Neall, *Biographical Sketches of the Bench and Bar of South Carolina* (Charleston: S. G. Courtenay & Co., 1859), Vol. II, p. 597.]

Scarbrough & Cooke		7 Broad street
Shirras, Alexander & Co.		29 Bay

Names	Occupations	Addresses
Simpson, John & William		27 Tradd street
Slann & Guignard		81 Tradd street
Smerdon, Henry		99 Broad street
Smith, John & Archibald		14 Broad street
Smith, Roger & Peter		101 Broad street
Smith, William	attorney	10 Broad street

[John Belton O'Neall, *Biographical Sketches of the Bench and Bar of Charleston* (Charleston: S. G. Courtenay & Co., 1859), Vol. II, p. 603.]

Names	Occupations	Addresses
Smiths, Desaussure & Darrell		83 Tradd street
Stevens, Daniel		15 Archdale street
Stevens, Ramsay & Co.		92½ Broad street
Stewart, Hayes, & Co.		11 Elliott street
Stewart, Robert and Hall		29 Bay
Teasdale, John & Co.		39 Bay
Thayer & Bartlet		Corner King & Queen streets
Thompson & Lennox		110 Broad street
Timothy, Ann		89 Broad street
Trescot, Edward		117 Meeting street
Tunno, Adam		82 Broad street
Van Rhyn & Newman		29 Bay
Villepontoux & Co.		Roper's wharf
Wadsworth & Porter		91 Broad street
Wakefield, James		88 Broad street
Walker, Alexander		88 Church street
Walker & Maitland		21 Church street
Ward, Samuel		4 Queen street
Webb & Doughty		111 Broad street
Wells & Bethune		10½ Broad street
Weyman, Edward		98 Church street
Wilkinson, Abraham & Co.		90 Broad street
Wilson, John & Co.		34 Bay
Winthrop, Todd & Winthrop		46 Bay

Glossary

This glossary is presented in an effort to help the reader understand some of the eighteenth century occupations. The sources and their short forms are listed below.

Johnson, Samuel, *A Dictionary of the English language: in which the words are deduced from their originals, and illustrated in their different significations by examples from the best writers. to which are prefixed a History of the language, and an English Grammar*. 2 vols. London: Printed by W. Strahan, for J. and P. Knapton; T. and T. Longman; C. Hitch and L. Harves; A. Millar; and R. and J. Dodsley, 1755-1756. Short form: Johnson, 1755-1756.

Johnson, Samuel, *A Dictionary of the English Language: in which the words are deduced from their originals, illustrated in their different significations by examples from the best writers, to which are prefixed a history of the language, and an English grammar*. 2 vols. Philadelphia: James Maxwell, 1819. Short form: Johnson, 1819.

Nadelhaft, Jerome J., *The Disorders of War: The Revolution in South Carolina*. Orono, Maine: University of Maine at Orono Press, 1981. Short form: Nadelhaft, Disorders.

The Oxford English Dictionary being a corrected re-issue with an introduction, supplement, and bibliography of a New English Dictionary on Historical Principles founded mainly on the materials collected by the Philological Society. 12 vols. Oxford: Clarendon Press, 1933; reprint, 1961. Short form: Oxford, 1961.

The Oxford English Dictionary being a corrected re-issue with an introduction, supplement, and bibliography of a New English Dictionary on Historical Principles founded mainly on the materials collected by the Philological Society. 12 vols. Oxford: Clarendon Press, 1933; reprint, 1970. Short form: Oxford, 1970.

Rogers, George C., Jr., *Charleston in the Age of the Pinckneys*. Norman: University of Oklahoma Press, 1969. Short form: Rogers, Charleston.

academy (1) An assembly or society of men, uniting for the promotion of some art. (2) The place were (*sic*) sciences are taught. (3) An university. (4) A place of education in contradistinction to the universities or public schools. Johnson, 1755-1756, Vol. I.

apothecary   A man whose business is to keep medicine for sale. Johnson, 1755-1756, Vol. I.

attorney   Such a person as by consent, commandment, or request, takes heed, fees, and takes upon him the charge of other men's business, in their absence.... Attorneys in common law are nearly the same with proctors in the civil law, and solicitors in courts of equity. Attorneys sue out writs or process, commence, carry on, and defend actions, or other proceedings, in the names of other persons, in the courts of common law. None are admitted to act without having served a clerkship for five years, taking the proper oath, being enrolled, and examined by the judges. Johnson, 1755-1756, Vol. I.

auctioneer   The person that manages an auction. Johnson, 1755-1756, Vol. I.

baker   One whose trade is to bake. Johnson, 1755-1756, Vol. I.

bandbox   A slight box used for bands and other things of small weight. Johnson, 1755-1756, Vol. I.

band box mak.   Band box maker. See band box.

banker   One that trafficks in money; one that keeps or manages a bank. Johnson, 1755-1756, Vol. I.

barber   One who shaves the beard. Johnson, 1755-1756, Vol. I.

barrister   A person qualified to plead causes, called an advocate or licentiate in other countries and courts. Outer barristers are pleaders without the bar, to distinguish them from inner barristers, such are the benchers, or those who have been readers, the counsel of the king, queen, or princes, who are admitted to plead within the bar. A counsellor at law. Johnson, 1755-1756, Vol. I.

beer house   A house licensed for the sale of beer, but not of spirits. Oxford, 1970, Vol. I, p. 759.

blacksmith   A smith that works in iron; so called from being very smutty. Johnson, 1755-1756, Vol. I.

boarding house   A house in which persons board. Oxford, 1970, Vol. I, p. 955.

boarding school   A school where the scholars live with the teacher. Johnson, 1755-1756, Vol. I.

bookbinder   A man whose profession is to bind books. Johnson, 1755-1756, Vol. I.

bookseller   A vender of books. Oxford, 1970, Vol. I, p. 992.

botantist   One skilled in plants; one who studies the various species of plants. Johnson, 1755-1756, Vol. I.

brewer   A man whose profession it is to make beer. Johnson, 1755-1756, Vol. I.

brick-burner   One who attends to a brick-kiln, a brick-maker. Oxford, 1970, Vol. I, p. 1093.

bricklayer   One whose trade is to build with bricks; a brick-mason. Johnson, 1755-1756, Vol. I. One who lays the brick in a building. Oxford, 1970, Vol. I, p. 1094.

brickmaker   See brick burner.

broker   A factor; one that does business for another; one that makes bargains for another. Johnson, 1755-1756, Vol. I.

butcher   One that kills animals to sell their flesh. Johnson, 1755-1756, Vol. I.

cabinet maker   One whose business is to make cabinets and the finer kind of joiner's work. Oxford, 1970, Vol. II, p. 6.

carpenter   An artificer in wood; a builder of houses and ships. He is distinguished from a joiner, as the carpenter performs larger and stronger work. Johnson, 1755-1756, Vol. I.

carter   The man who drives a cart, or whose trade it is to drive a cart. Johnson, 1755-1756, Vol. I.

carver   A sculptor. Johnson, 1755-1756, Vol. I.

cashier   He that has charge of the money. Johnson, 1755-1756, Vol. I.

chancellor   The title of certain judges of courts of chancery or equity, established by the statutes of separate states. Oxford, 1970, Vol. II, p. 265.

chandler   An artisan whose trade it is to make candles, or a person who sells them. Johnson, 1755-1756, Vol. I.

clerk   (1) A clergyman. (2) A scholar; a man of letters. (3) A man employed under another as a writer. (4) A petty writer in publick offices; an officer of various kind. Johnson, 1755-1756, Vol. I. In early times, when writing was not an ordinary accomplishment of the laity, the offices of writer, scribe, secretary, keeper of accounts, and the transaction of all business involving writing, were discharged by clerks. Oxford, 1970, Vol. II, p. 493.

coachmaker   The artificer whose trade is to make coaches. Johnson, 1755-1756, Vol. I.

coffee house   A house of entertainment where coffee is sold, and the guests are supplied with a newspaper. Johnson, 1755-1756, Vol. I.

comedian   (1) A player or actor of comic parts. (2) A player in general: a stage-player; an actress or actor. (3) A writer of comedies. Johnson, 1819, Vol. I.

commandant   A commanding officer, a commander: irrespective of rank. Oxford, 1970, Vol. II, p. 669.

commissary   An officer made occasionally for a certain purpose; a delegate; a deputy. Johnson, 1755-1756, Vol. I.

confectioner   One whose trade is to make confections or sweetmeats. Johnson, 1755-1756, Vol. I.

constable   An officer of the peace. Oxford, 1970, Vol. II, p. 872.

cooper   One who makes coops or barrels. Johnson, 1755-1756, Vol. I.

coroner   An officer whose duty is to enquire, on the part of the king, how any violent death was occasioned; for which purpose a jury of twelve persons is empannelled. Johnson, 1755-1756, Vol. I.

counsellor   One that gives advice. Johnson, 1755-1756, Vol. I.

currier   One who dresses and pares leather for those who make shoes, or other things. Johnson, 1755-1756, Vol. I.

custom house   The house where the taxes upon goods imported or exported are collected. Johnson, 1755-1756, Vol. I.

cutler   One who makes or sell knives. Johnson, 1755-1756, Vol. I.

deputy   A lieutenant; a viceroy; one that is appointed by a special commission to govern and act instead of another. Johnson, 1755-1756, Vol.

I.

distill (1) To drop; to fall by drops. (2) To flow gently and silently. (3) To use a still; to practice the act of distillation. Johnson, 1755-1756, Vol. I.

distiller One who practices the trade of distilling. Johnson, 1755-1756, Vol. I.

doctor (1) One that has taken the highest degree in faculties of divinity, law, or physick. In some universities they have doctors of musick. In its original import, it means a man so well versed in his faculty, as to be qualified to teach it. (2) A man skilled in any profession. (3) A physician; one who undertakes the cure of diseases. (4) Any able or learned man. Johnson, 1819, Vol. I.

dray The cart on which beer is sold. Johnson, 1755-1756, Vol. I.

drayman One that attends a dray or cart. Johnson, 1755-1756, Vol. I.

dunner One employed in soliciting petty debts. Johnson, 1819, Vol. I.

dyer One whose occupation is to dye cloth and other materials. Oxford, 1970, Vol. III, p. 735.

engraver A cutter in stone or other matter. Johnson, 1755-1756, Vol. I.

Esq. Esquire.

esquire A man belonging to the higher order of English gentry, ranking immediately below a knight. (2) A landed proprietor, (country) 'squire. As a title accompanying a man's name, originally applied to those who were 'esquires' in sense 2; subsequently extended to other persons to whom an equivalent degree of rank or status is by courtesy attributed. Oxford, 1961, Vol. III, p 292.

factor An agent for another; one who transacts business for another. Commonly a substitute in mercantile affairs. Johnson, 1755-1756, Vol. I.

fisherman One whose employment and livelihood is to catch fish. Johnson, 1755-1756, Vol. I.

farmer (1) One who cultivates hired ground. (2) One who cultivates ground, whether his own or another's. Johnson, 1755-1756, Vol. I.

gaol A prison; a place of confinement. Johnson, 1755-1756, Vol. I.

gardener He that attends or cultivates gardens. Johnson, 1755-1756, Vol. I.

gauger One whose business is to measure vessels or quantities. Johnson, 1755-1756, Vol. I.

gilder One who lays gold on the surface of any other body. Johnson, 1755-1756, Vol. I.

glazier One whose trade is to make glass windows. Other manufacturers of glass are otherwise named. Johnson, 1755-1756, Vol. I.

goldsmith (1) One who manufactures gold. (2) A banker; one who keeps money for others in his hands. Johnson, 1755-1756, Vol. I.

grocer Originally being one who dealt by wholesale. A grocer is a man who buys and sells tea, sugar and plums and spices for gain. Johnson, 1755-1756, Vol. I.

gunsmith A man whose trade is to make guns. Johnson, 1755-1756, Vol. I.

hackney coach A four-wheeled coach, drawn by two horses, and seated for six persons, kept for hire. Oxford, 1970, Vol. V, p. 12.

hair dresser   One whose business is to dress and cut the hair. Oxford, 1970, Vol. V, p. 25.

hatter   A maker of hats. Johnson, 1755-1756, Vol. I.

hotel   A house for the entertainment of strangers and travellers, an inn; *esp.* one that is, or claims to be, of a superior kind. Oxford, 1961, Vol. V, p. 412.

innholder   A man who keeps an inn; an innkeeper. Johnson, 1755-1756, Vol. I.

inspector   (1) A prying examiner. (2) A superintendent. Johnson, 1755-1756, Vol. I.

intendant   An officer of the highest class, who oversees any particular allotment of the publick business. Johnson, 1755-1756, Vol. I. An official of the City of Charleston under the corporation of 1783. Rogers, Charleston, p. 51.

ironmonger   A dealer in iron. Johnson, 1755-1756, Vol. I.

jailer   A gaoler; the keeper of a prison. Johnson, 1755-1756, Vol. I.

jeweller   One who trafficks in precious stones. Johnson, 1755-1756, Vol. I.

jobber   A man who sells stocks in the publick funds. Johnson, 1755-1756, Vol. I.

joiner   One whose trade is to make utensils of wood joined. Johnson, 1755-1756, Vol. I.

land surveyor   One whose professional occupation is to measure land, draw up plans of estates, and the like. Oxford, 1970, Vol. VI, p. 55.

leatherdresser   He who dresses leather. Johnson, 1755-1756, Vol. II.

librarian   One who has the care of a library. (2) One who transcribes or copies books. Johnson, 1755-1756, Vol. II.

limner   A painter; a picture-maker. Johnson, 1755-1756, Vol. II.

livery stable   A stable where horses are kept at livery, or are let out (with or without carriages) for hire. Oxford, 1970, Vol. VI, p. 364.

mantuamaker   One who makes gowns for women. Johnson, 1755-1756, Vol. II.

mariner   A seaman; a sailor. Johnson, 1755-1756, Vol. II.

merchant   One who trafficks to remote countries. Johnson, 1755-1756, Vol. II.

messenger   One who carries an errand; one who comes from another to a third; one who brings an account or foretoken of any thing; an harbinger; a forerunner. Johnson, 1755-1756, Vol. II.

midwife   A woman who assists women in childbirth. Johnson, 1755-1756, Vol. II.

millener   See milliner.

milliner   One who sells ribands and dresses for women. Johnson, 1755-1756, Vol. II.

miniat. paint.   Miniature painter.

minister   (1) An agent; one who is employed to any end; one who acts not by any inherent authority, but under another. (2) One who is employed in the administration of government. (3) One who serves at the altar; one who performs sacerdotal functions. (4) A delegate; an official. (5) An agent from a foreign power, without the dignity of an ambassador. Johnson, 1755-1756, Vol. II.

notary   An officer whose business it is to take notes of any thing which may concern the publick. Johnson, 1755-1756, Vol. II.

overseer To superintend; to overlook. Johnson, 1755-1756, Vol. II.

painter One who perfects the art of representing objects by colours. Johnson, 1755-1756, Vol. II.

perfumer One whose trade is to sell things made to gratify the scent. Johnson, 1755-1756, Vol. II.

physician One who professes the art of healing. Johnson, 1755-1756, Vol. II.

pilot He whose office is to steer the ship. Johnson, 1755-1756, Vol. II.

planter (1) One who sows, sets or cultivates ground in the West Indian colonies. Johnson, 1755-1756, Vol. II.

poorhouse A house in which poor people in receipt of public charity are lodged; a workhouse. Oxford, 1970, Vol. VII, p. 1115.

porterhouse A house at which porter and other malt liquors are retailed. Oxford, 1970, Vol. VII, p. 1143.

postmaster One who has charge of publick conveyance of letters. Johnson, 1755-1756, Vol. II.

printer One that prints book. Johnson, 1755-1756, Vol. II.

professor One who declares himself of an opinion or party. (2) One who publickly practices or teaches art. Johnson, 1755-1756, Vol. II.

R. rector.

rabbi A doctor among the Jews. Johnson, 1755-1756, Vol. II.

rector Parson of an unimpropriated parish. Johnson, 1755-1756, Vol. II.

register The officer whose business is to write and keep the register. Johnson, 1755-1756, Vol. II.

retailer One who sells by small quantities. Johnson, 1755-1756, Vol. II.

ropemaker One who makes rope to sell. Johnson, 1755-1756, Vol. II.

runner A messenger. Johnson, 1755-1756, Vol. II.

saddler One whose trade is to make saddles. Johnson, 1755-1756, Vol. II.

sawyer One whose trade is to saw lumber into boards or beams. Johnson, 1755-1756, Vol. II.

schoolmaster One who presides and teaches in a school. Johnson, 1755-1756, Vol. II.

schoolmistress A woman who governs a school. Johnson, 1755-1756, Vol. II.

scrivener One who draws contracts. Johnson, 1755-1756, Vol. II.

seaman A sailor; a navigator; a mariner. Johnson, 1755-1756, Vol. II.

seamstress A woman who seams or sews; a needlewoman whose occupation is plain sewing as distinguished from dress or mantlemaking, decorative embroidery, etc. Oxford, 1970, Vol. IX, p. 330.

secretary One intrusted with the management of businesses; one who writes for another. Johnson, 1819, Vol. II.

seedsman The sower; he that scatters the seed. Johnson, 1755-1756, Vol. II.

sheriff An officer to whom is intrusted in each county the execution of the laws. Johnson, 1755-1756, Vol. II.

ship carpenter A carpenter employed in the building or repairing of ships. Oxford, 1970, Vol. IX, p. 708.

ship chandler A dealer who supplies ships with necessary stores. Oxford,

1970, Vol. IX, p. 708.

shipmaster   Master of the ship. Johnson, 1755-1756, Vol. II.

shipwright   A builder of ships. Johnson, 1755-1756, Vol. II.

shoemaker   One whose trade is to make shoes. Oxford, 1970, Vol. IX, p. 726.

shopkeeper   A trader who sells in a shop; not a merchant who only deals by wholesale. Johnson, 1755-1756, Vol. II.

silversmith   One that works in silver. Johnson, 1755-1756, Vol. II.

starch   A kind of viscous matter made of flower or potatoes, with which linen is stiffened, and was formerly coloured. Johnson, 1755-1756, Vol. II.

starcher   One whose trade is to starch. Johnson, 1755-1756, Vol. II.

stationer   (1) A bookseller. (2) A seller of paper. Johnson, 1755-1756, Vol. II.

stay   A large rope used to support a mast, and leading from its head down to some other mast or spar, or to some part of the ship. Oxford, 1970, Vol. X, p. 872.

stay maker   See stay.

stock jobber   A low wretch who gets money by buying and selling shares in the funds. Johnson, 1755-1756, Vol. II.

stone cutter   One whose trade is to hew stones. Johnson, 1755-1756, Vol. II.

storekeeper   One who has charge of a store or stores; one who superintends the receipt and issue of stores; spec. an officer in charge of naval or military stores. Oxford, 1970, Vol. X, p. 1036.

sugarbaker   A confectioner. Oxford, 1970, Vol. X, p. 116.

surgeon   One who cures by manual operation; one whose duty is to act in external maladies by the direction of the physician. Johnson, 1755-1756, Vol. II.

surveyor   An overseer; one placed to superintend others. Johnson, 1755-1756, Vol. II.

tailor   One whose business is to make clothes. Johnson, 1819, Vol. II.

tallowchandler   One who makes candles of tallow, not of wax. Johnson, 1755-1756, Vol. II.

tanner   One whose trade is to tan leather. Johnson, 1755-1756, Vol. II.

tavern   A house where wine is sold, and drinkers are entertained. Johnson, 1755-1756, Vol. II.

tavern keeper   One who keeps a tavern. Johnson, 1755-1756, Vol. II.

taylor   See tailor.

tinman   A manufacturer of tin; or iron tinned over. Johnson, 1755-1756, Vol. II.

tobacconist   A preparer and vender of tobacco. Johnson, 1755-1756, Vol. II.

turner   One whose trade is turn in a lathe. Johnson, 1755-1756, Vol. II.

undertaker   (1) One who engages in projects and affairs. (2) One who engages to build for another at a certain price. (3) One who manages funerals. Johnson, 1755-1756, Vol. II.

upholsterer   One who furnishes houses; one who fits up apartments with beds and furniture. Johnson, 1755-1756, Vol. II.

vendue masters   They sold at public auction secondhand goods belonging to
   persons attempting to raise cash quickly, property owned by people involved
   in bankruptcy proceedings, and property ordered sold by the court of chancery. Auctioneers were required by the government to secure licenses,
   give bonded security, and pay a tax of 2½ per cent, one-half their commission on almost all the goods they sold. Nedelhaft, *Disorders*, pp.
   119-120.

vinter   One who sells wine. Johnson, 1755-1756, Vol. II.

waiter   An attendant; one who attends for the accommodations of others.
   Johnson, 1755-1756, Vol. II.

warden   One of the governing officials of the City of Charleston under the
   corporation of 1783. Rogers, *Charleston*, p. 51.

watchmaker   One whose trade is to make watches, or pocket clocks. Johnson,
   1755-1756, Vol. II.

wharf.   Wharfinger.

wharfinger   One who attends a wharf. Johnson, 1755-1756, Vol. II. An owner
   or keeper of a wharf. Oxford, 1970, Vol. XII, p. 5

wheelwright   A maker of wheel carriages. Johnson, 1755-1756, Vol. II.

Bibliography

Acheson, Patricia C. *America's Colonial Heritage*. New York: Dodd, Mead & Company, 1957.

Barnett, A. Elzas, M.D., L.L.D. *The Jews of South Carolina from the earliest times to the present day*. Philadelphia: J. B. Lippincott Company, 1905.

Bowes, Frederick P. *The Culture of Early Charleston*. Chapel Hill: The University of North Carolina Press, 1942.

Cohen, Hennig. *The South Carolina Gazette, 1732-1775*. Columbia: The University of South Carolina Press, 1953.

Johnson, Samuel. *A Dictionary of the English language: in which the words are deduced from their originals, and illustrated in their different significations by examples from the best writers. to which are prefixed a History of the language, and an English Grammar*. 2 vols. London: Printed by W. Strahan, for J. and P. Knapton; T. and T. Longman; C. Hitch and L. Harves; A. Millar; and R. and J. Dodsley, 1755-1756.

Johnson, Samuel. *A Dictionary of the English Language: in which the words are deduced from their originals, illustrated in their different significations by examples from the best writers, to which are prefixed a history of the language, and an English grammar*. 2 vols. Philadelphia: James Maxwell, 1819.

McCowen, George Smith, Jr. *The British Occupation of Charleston, 1780-82*. Columbia: The University of South Carolina Press, 1972.

Milligan, Jacob. *The Charleston Directory*. Charleston: W. P. Young, 1794.

___, *The Charleston Directory; and Revenue System of the United States*. Charleston: T. B. Bowen, 1790.

Nadelhaft, Jerome J. *The Disorders of War: The Revolution in South Carolina*. Orono, Maine: University of Maine at Orono Press, 1981.

The Oxford English Dictionary being a corrected re-issue with an introduction, supplement, and bibliography of a New English Dictionary on Historical Principles founded mainly on the materials collected by the Philological Society. 12 vols. Oxford: Clarendon Press, 1933; reprint, 1961.

The Oxford English Dictionary being a corrected re-issue with an introduction, supplement, and bibliography of a New English Dictionary on Historical Principles founded mainly on the materials collected by the Philological Society. 12 vols. Oxford: Clarendon Press, 1933, reprint, 1970.

Rogers, George C., Jr. *Charleston in the Age of the Pinckneys*. Norman: University of Oklahoma Press, 1969.

Tobler, John. *The South Carolina and Georgia Alamack for 1785*. 1784.

___, *The South Carolina and Georgia Almanack, for the year of our Lord 1782; Being second, after LEAP-YEAR. CONTAINING The Lunations; Eclipses; Rising and Setting of the Moon and Stars; Aspects; Judgment of the Weather; &c. &c. &c.* Charlestown: R. Wells & Son.

Wright, Louis B. *The Cultural Life of the American Colonies*. New York:

Harper & Brothers, 1957.

Index

Binnie, William, 7
Bird, Elizabeth, 93
Bird, Reading, 19
Bisbane, James, 86
Bithouse, John, 44
Biverly, Frederick, 33
Black, John, 33, 44
Black, Nathaniel, 33, 89
Blackaller, Oliver, 33, 44
Blackie, Elizabeth, 99
Blacklock, William, 33, 44
Blacklock & Tunno, 105
Blair, James, 99
Blair, James & Co., 29
Blair, John, 33
Blair, William, 86
Blake, Edward, 33, 44
Blake, Elizabeth, 54
Blake, John, 33, 44
Blakeley, Samuel, 44
Blakely, David, 29
Blakely, Samuel, 33, 105
Blamyer, William, 9, 99
Bleakly, Archibald, 105
Bochet & Co., 65
Bocquet, Peter, 55
Boddie, Sarah, 64
Boderum, Joseph, 93
Bodie, Sarah, 65
Bogie, Agnes, 93
Bohm, Charles, 64
Boibliat, Peter, 80
Boiler, Joseph, 19
Bold, Rhodes & Co., 33, 44
Bollough, Mary, 99
Bolton, Martha, 93
Bonetheau, John, 89
Bonetheau, Peter, 89
Bonfall, Samuel, 19
Bonfell, Samuel, 55
Bonneau, Francis, 9, 19
Boomer, John, 105
Booner, Christian, 33, 44
Booner, Dolly, 93
Booth, Catharine, 64, 65
Boothe, Thomas, 19
Border, Mary, 44
Boswell, James, 19
Boucheuneau, Charles, 93

Bouchonneau, Charles, 99
Boulliat, Peter, 82
Bounetheau, John, 87
Bounetheau, Peter, 87, 105
Bounnetheau, Peter, 87
Bourdeaux, Daniel, 33, 44
Bourdeaux, Daniel & Co., 105
Bouteille, Jean, 82
Bowen, Thomas B., 9
Bowen & Elliott, 19
Bowen & Harrison, 19
Bowen & Markland, 105
Bower, Katharine, 105
Bower, William, 7
Bowing, George, 93
Bowman, John, 55, 57
Boyce, Katharine, 7
Boyd, Elizabeth, 99
Boyerle, Frederick, 44
Bradford, Charles, 64
Bradford, Charles & Co., 44
Bradford, Thomas, 19, 61
Bradford, William, 33
Bradford & Co., 44
Brady, Mary, 95
Brailsford, John, 44
Brailsford, Samuel, 44, 95
Brailsford, William, 55, 105
Brally, Thomas, 19
Braly, Thomas, 33
Brandford, Elizabeth, 95
Branford, Elizabeth, 99
Bremar, Francis, 87, 89
Bricken, Sarah, 61, 65
Briendly, Stephen, 80
Brindley, Stephen, 82
Brodie, Robert, 19
Brodie, Thomas, 33, 44
Brook, Mary, 95
Brooke, Charles, 44
Broughton, Ann, 55, 99
Brower, Jeremiah, 95, 99
Brown, Mrs. ___, 71
Brown, Squire ___, 19
Brown, Clarkson, & Co., 29
Brown, Daniel, 82
Brown, James, 7, 44, 95
Brown, Jeremiah, 80, 105
Brown, Joseph, 55, 99

Canty, Henry & Co., 44
Canty and Solomons, 33
Cap, Dominick, 80
Cape, Brian, 30, 44
Cape, Bryan, 33
Carne, Samuel, 30
Carner, Lawrence, 33
Carnes, John, 70
Carnes, Susannah, 95
Carolan, Philip, 71
Carpenter, James, 33, 44
Carr, Wilder & Co., 34
Carr & Firby, 44
Carradeaux, General ___, 89
Carrel, Daniel, 9
Carrell, Daniel, 19
Carson, Elizabeth, 95
Carson, James, 9, 44
Carson, William, 57
Carson, William & James, 30
Cart, John, 44
Cart, John, junior, 95
Cart, John, senior, 95
Cart, John & Co., 106
Cart, Joseph, 19
Cart, Sarah, 100
Carter, George, 70, 71
Carter, Dr. George, 70
Carter, John, 34
Cartmell, William, 34
Cartwright, Paul, 100
Casey, Benjamin, 19
Castine, John, 9
Cavaneau, James, 34
Caveneau, Elizabeth, 9
Caveneau, James, 19
Cazeneau, Edward, 34
Chalmers, Eliza, 95, 100
Chalmers, Gilbert, 9
Chalmers, Rebecca, 95
Chambers, Gilbert, 19
Chambers, John, 30
Champney, John, 34
Champneys, John, 57
Chandler, Dr. Isaac, 106
Chandler & Marshall, 71
Chanler, Isaac, 70
Chapman, William, 9
Charles, Andrew, 44

Charles, Henry, 20
Charles, James, 9, 20
Chevers, Alexander, 45
Cheves, Alexander, 34
Childs, Nathan & Co., 106
Chion, P. G. and Son, 34
Chion, Peter G. & Son, 45
Chisholm, Alex., junior, 34
Chisholm, Alexander, 55
Chisolm, Alexander, 30, 58
Chitty, Ann, 45, 95
Chouler, Joseph, 71
Chriestzburgh, Michael, 20
Christian, Elizabeth, 100
Christian, Robert, 64
Christie, Alexander, 9, 20
Christie, Edward, 34, 45, 89
Chupein, Lewis, 9, 20
Clark, Francis-Rush, 86
Clark, Jeremiah, 9
Clark, John, 9, 95
Clark, Sarah, 34
Clark, William, 9
Clarke, Benjamin, 20
Clarke, David, 20
Clarke, James, 9, 20
Clarke, Jeremiah, 89
Clarke, John, 9, 20, 45
Clarke, Mary, 34, 100
Clarke, William, 20
Clarke and Latham, 9
Clarkson, Alexander, 9
Clastier, Maxemellian, 20
Cleary, John R., 62
Clement, John, 20
Clements, John, 9
Clementson, Alexander, 87
Clifford, Elizabeth, 95
Clime, Mary, 95
Clitheral, James, 70
Clitherall, James, 71
Clitherall, Dr. James, 70
Coates, Thomas, 80
Coats, Thomas, 65
Cobham, George, 106
Cobia, Daniel, 9
Cobia, Elizabeth, 100
Cobia, Francis, 9
Cobia, Margaret, 100

Crookshanks, Daniel, 20
Crookshanks, William, 20
Cross, George, 34, 45
Cross, James, 100
Cross, Susannah, 95
Cross & Crawlay, 45
Crowe, Edward, 87, 89
Crowley, Charles, 34
Crowley, Michael, 34
Cruden, John, 30
Cruger, David Frederick, 45
Cruger, Frederick D., 34
Cudworth, Benjamin, 106
Cudworth, Nathaniel, 95, 100
Cudworth, Waller, 106
Cughan, George, 10
Cumin, Casper, 95
Cummings, Janet, 71
Cunaghar, Thomas, 45
Cunningham, John, 34, 45
Cunnington, William, 89, 106
Cuppage, Hugh, 80
Curling, Thomas, 34, 45
Currie & Norris, 73
Curry, William, 34, 80
Curtis, ___, 20
Custer, James, 95, 100
Custom house & naval office, 95
Cyples, Margaret, 100

Dacosta, Isaac, 34, 45
Dacosta, Joseph, 45
Dacosta, Samuel, 34
Dacosta, Sarah, 95
Dallas, Angus, 34
Daniel, Elizabeth, 95, 100
Darby, William, 10
Darrell, Benjamin, 80, 82
Darrell, Edward, 34, 45
Darrell, Edward, junior, 77
Dart, Mrs. ___, 100
Dart, Benjamin, 30
Dart, Isaac Motte, 77
Dart, John Sandford, 87, 89
Dater, rev. Frederick, 68
Davidson, Gilbert & J., 45
Davie, William, 30, 95, 100

Davis, Jane, 10, 45
Davis, John Maynard, 45
Davis, L. H., 76
Davis, Lightfoot H., 77
Davis, Thomas, 34, 45
Dawes, Margaret, 95
Dawes, Ralph, 106
Dawson, Mrs. Christian, 93
Dawson, Christiana, 64, 65
Dawson, John, 45, 55, 58
Dawson, Michael, 87
Day, George, 20
Dazivido, Isaac, 45
Deady, Thomas, 35, 45
Dearlon, Martin, 45
Deas, Elizabeth, 100
Deas, John, 55, 93
Deas, John, junior, 55
Deas, William, 76
Debow, John, 20
Delcor, Peter, 35
Delorme, Francis, 20
Decker, William & Co., 35
Delavergene, ___, 100
Delyon, Isaac, 35, 100
Dener, George, 10, 20
Dener, Peter, 10, 20
Dennis, Richard, 35
Denny, Samuel, 20
Denoon, David & co., 74
Denoon, David & Co., 74
Denton, James, 65, 95
Depass, Ralph, 74
Depeyster, ___, 100
Desaussure, Daniel, 35, 45
Desaussure, H. William, 76
Desaussure, Henry Wm., 77
Desaussure, William H., 87
Desaussure & Ford, 77
Desaussure & Greaves, 45
Desel, Charles, 10
Desell, Charles, 20
Desverneys, Anthony P., 20
Deveaux, Jacob, 45, 86
Deveaux, Jacob & son, 46
Devernay, Peter F., 10
Devona, ___, 100
Dewar, Robert, 58, 95
Dewees, Sarah, 95

Dewees, William, 35, 46
Dickenson, Francis, 77
Dickenson, Jeremiah, 80, 82
Dickenson, Joseph, 20
Dickson, Samuel, 61, 62
Dill, Joseph, 10
Dill, Joseph, junior, 46
Dill, Joseph, senior, 20
Dillon & Chisselle, 106
Dimes, Ann, 61
Disher, Mary, 95, 100
Ditcham, John, 80
Dodge, Joseph, 20
Dodsworth, Ralph, 35, 46
Doggett, Henry, 74
Dollaghan & Brannen, 35
Donaldson, James, 7, 10, 20
Donaldson, Mary, 100
Donavan, James, 10
Dorman, Robert, 35
Dorrill, Robert, 46
Dougharty, Patrick, 20
Dougherty, Patrick, 10
Doughty, Abraham, 95
Doughty, Thomas, 7, 35, 46, 106
Doughty, William, 55, 58,, 106
Douglas, Joseph, 35
Douglas, Nathaniel, 35
Douglass, Nat. & John, 46
Douxsaint, Mary Esther, 95
Douxsaint, William, 48
Dow, Alexander, 30
Down, James, 46
Downe, James, 35
Downes, Arthur, 93
Downey, Mrs. ___, 100
D'Oyley, Ann, 100
Drayton, Jacob, 76, 77
Drayton, John, 76, 77
Drayton, Rebecca, 96
Drayton, Stephen, 87
Drayton, Thomas, 58
Drayton & Stevens, 106
Drummond, Ann, 100
Drummond, John, 20
Drysdale, Alexander, 30
Dubald, Frederick, 100
Dubnard, Peter, 20
Dubuard, Peter, 10

Duff, David, 61
Duff, John, 10
Duffy, Andrew, 35, 46
Duffy, James, 46
Dulles, Joseph, 35, 46
Duncan, ___, 20
Duncan, Archibald, 10
Duncan, George, 30
Duncan, James, 7, 10, 20
Duncan, Patrick, 35
Duncan, Thomas, 10
Duncan & Murdock, 20
Dunn, Alexander, 20
Duntze, Gerard, 35
Dupont, Gideon, 30
Dupre, Benjamin, 20
DuPre, Cornelius, 106
Durang, ___, 100
Dursse, John, 100
Duval, Catharine, 96
Duvall, Catherine, 100
Dwight, Isaac, 35

Eames, Martha, 35
Earnest, Jacob, 10
Ears, William, 80
Easton, Susannah, 96
Ebberly, John, 20
Eberly, John, 10
Echlar, Christopher, 20
Eckhard, Jacob, 61
Eckhart, Jacob, 62
Edean, Joshua, 21
Eden, Joshua, 10
Edgeworth, John, 10
Edwards, Alexander, 76, 77
Edwards, James, 30, 35, 46, 106
Edwards, John, 35, 74, 96
Edwards, Edward & Co., 35
Ehny, Catharine, 100
Ehrick & Reynolds, 46
Eldridge, Randall, 80
Elfe, Thomas, 21
Elliott, Elizabeth, 96
Elliott, Thomas, 55, 58
Elliott, Thomas O., 55
Elliott, Thomas Odinfell, 58

Ellis, John, 80
Ellis, Thomas, 21
Ellison and Dupont, 106
Ellsinore, James, 106
Elmore, Jeffy, 21
Elmore, Jesse, 10
Elsinore, James, 87
Elsworth, Theophilus, 87, 89
Emanuel, Joseph, 10
Emmet, Charlotte, 96
English, Thomas, 46
Evans, George, 55
Eveleigh, Thomas, 55
Eveleigh, Thomas & Co., 106
Ewing, Adam, 35, 46
Ewing, John, 7
Ewing, Robert, 35
Ewing, Robert & Adam, 46
Eyers, Thomas, 21
Eyers, William, 82

Fabert, Joseph, 46
Fabre, John, rev., 68
Fabre, John, Rev. C., 68
Fabre & Price, 35
Fair, William, 10, 21, 35, 46
Fairchild, Aaron, 21
Fardo, George, 30, 35
Farguhar, Robert & Co., 30
Farquahar, John, 96
Farr, Joseph, 55
Farr, Thomas, 106
Farrow, William, 80
Fayssoux, Peter, 70, 71
Felix, Frederick, 10
Fell, Elizabeth, 21
Fell, Thomas, 7, 35
Fereaud, Alexander, 100
Ferguson, Mrs. ___, 100
Ferguson, Ann, 96
Ferguson, Charles, 106
Ferril, Anthony, 10
Fiddy, Wiliam, 35, 46
Fields, John, 35, 46
Fields, William Brown, 46
Fife, James, 21
Filbin, Charles, 58

Finlayson, Mrs. ___, 21
Finlayson, John, 10
Finlayson, Mungo, 10
Fishburne, William, 55
Fisher, George, 10
Fisher, James, 46
Fisher, John, 7
Fisher & Berney, 35
Fisher, Hughes & Edwards, 106
Fitzhipps, John, 35
Fitzpatrick, John, 35
Flagg, George, 58, 106
Flagg, Henry Collins, 71
Flagg, Dr. Henry-Collins, 106
Flagg, Samuel Hort, 71
Fleming, John, 10
Flemming, John, 89
Flemming, Robert, 46
Fletcher, Phoebe, 96
Flin, Joseph, 35
Flint, Joseph, 46
Florin, Lucas, 100
Florine, Lucas, 96
Fluitt, Samuel, 35
Fogartie, Mary, 61, 62
Folker, Gaspar, 10
Folker, John Casper, 21, 106
Fonspertuis, Citizen ___, 89
Forbes, Elizabeth, 100
Ford, Bartholomew, 10
Ford, J., 76
Ford, Mary, 96
Ford, Timothy, 77
Fordham, Richard, 10, 21
Forrest, George, 35, 46
Forrest, Michael, 61, 100
Forrester, William, 80
Foskey, Bryan, 35
Foster, Thomas, 35, 100
Foster, Thomas & Seth, 30
Fowke, Chandler D., 76
Fowke, Chandler Din., 77
Fowler, Richard, 21
Fowler & Brodie, 21
Fraser, ___, 100
Fraser, Alexander, 55
Fraser, Charlie, 86
Fraser, James, 86
Fraser, John, 89

Good, Sarah, 61, 65
Goodwin, Robert, 11
Gordon, Andrew, 21
Gordon, James, 21, 30, 36, 46
Gordon, John, 36, 46, 80
Gordon, Mary, 96
Gordon, Thomas, 46, 101
Gordon, Thomas-Knox, 93
Gottier, Francis, 7
Gottier, Isabella, 96
Gould, John, 46
Gourlay, John, 21
Gowdey, William, 106
Graaf, Sibells, Brasselman & Co., 107
Graeme, Ann, 96
Graeser, Conrad Jacob, 36, 46
Graff & Co., 36
Graff, Seibels & co., 46
Graham, Mary, 71, 96
Graham, Richard, 36
Graham, Samuel, 11, 21, 46
Graham, William, 101
Grainger, James, 21
Granger, Thomas, 30
Grant, Alexander, 11, 21
Grant, Hary, 36, 89
Grant, John, 7, 11, 30
Grant, Lewis, 36
Grant & Kemmel, 7
Grant & Simons, 107
Granville, James, 21
Grassell, George, 21
Grattan, Francis, 107
Gratten, Daniel, 101
Gratton, Daniel, 30
Gravanstine, Frederick, 11, 21
Graves, Charles, 46
Graves, James, 11
Gray, Col. ___, 86
Gray, Benjamin, 36, 58
Gready, James, 11
Green, William, 36, 46
Greenhill, Hugh & Co., 11
Greenland, Daniel, 36
Greenland, George, 36, 47
Greenwood, Robert, 47
Greenwood, William, 36
Greenwood, Wm., junior, 47
Greenwood, Wm., senior, 47

Greenwood & Legge, 30
Greerly, Joseph, 21
Gregorie, James, 107
Gregorie, Douglas & Co., 30
Gregorie, James & son, 47
Gregorie son & Davidson, 36
Gregson, Thomas, 11
Grenville, James, 11
Gressel, George, 11
Grierson, James, 36, 47
Griggs, John, 36
Grimes, Mary, 36
Grimbal, Mary M., 101
Grimball, C. Isaac, 55
GRimke, John F., 87, 89
Grimke, John-Faucheraud, 107
Grimke, John Paul, 96, 107
Grimke, Mary, 101
Gross, Charles, 11
Grossman, Francis, 101
Grott, Francis, 11
Gruber, Charles, 11
Gruber, Charles, junior, 101
Gruber, Charles, senior, 21
Gruber, Samuel, 21
Gruly, Joseph, 11
Guerard, His Excellency Benja., 107
Guerard, Mary Ann, 96, 101
Guillaud, Claudius, 21
Guilleaud, Claudius, 11
Guirey, Elizabeth, 47
Gunn, William, 11, 21
Gury, Charles F., 101
Guy, James, 11, 21

Hadden, Gardner, 21
Hahnbaüm, Christian, 70
Hahnbaum, Dr. George, 107
Haig, Mrs. ___, 101
Haig, David, 21
Haig, Mary, 96
Haig & Dunn, 11, 22
Haig & Murray, 22
Haindsdorff, Henry, 11
Hains, Heath, 11
Hainsdorf, Henry, 22
Hair, Edward, 101

Heyward, Hannah, 101
Heyward, Nathaniel, 55, 58
Heyward, Thomas, jun., 58
Heyward, Thomas, sen., 58
Hilagers, George A., 37
Hill, Charles, 101
Hill, Duncan, 80, 82
Hill, Eleanor, 96
Hill, Jonathan, 22
Hill, Joseph, 96
Hill, Paul, 22, 37
Hill, Thomas, 47
Hillegas, George, 47
Hillegas, Joseph, 65
Hillegas, Philip, 37, 47
Hilligas, Jacob, 37
Himelie, John James, 22
Himili, James, 12
Hinds, Patrick, 7, 12, 22
Hinds, Thomas, 77
Hinlen, Thomas, 55
Hinson, Thomas, 37
Hirreld, George, 12
Hislop & Snowden, 37
Hobart, John, 22
Hodson, Margaret, 64
Hogan, David Henry, 80
Hogarth, William, 12
Hogsden, Mary, 22
Holbeck, John, 12
Holinshead, William, 68
Holland, Hugh, 12
Hollaway & Thayer, 37
Hollingshead, Rev. W^{m}., 68
Holmes, Isaac, 87, 90
Holmes, John B., 76, 87, 90
Holmes, John Bee, 90
Holmes Thomas, 12, 22
Holmes, William, 74
Holt, William, 12
Honeywood, Arthur, 12
Honeywood, Elizabeth, 22
Hook, George, 12
Hooper, Thomas & Co., 93
Hope, Mary, 96
Hope, Thomas, 12
Hopton, Sarah, 96
Hopton, William, 93
Horlbeck, John, 22

Hornby, Thomas, 22
Hornby, William, 7
Hornley, Thomas, 12
Horry, Thomas, 55, 58
Horsey, Thomas, 101
Hort, William, 87, 90
Hort & Warley, 107
Horton, Thomas, 37
Hostige, John, 37
Houckgeest, A. E. Van Braam, 107
Houlton, James, 101
House, Mary Ann, 37
House, Samuel, 47, 96
Hover, John, 12
Howard, Ann, 101
Howard, John, 22
Howard, Robert, 37
Howell, John, 12, 87
Hoyland, Ann Maria, 61, 62
Hrabowski, Ann, 47
Hubert, Barry, 37
Hubert, Charles, 37
Huck, Michael, 22
Hudson, Mary, 12
Hugeley, John, 37
Huger, Daniel Lionel, 90
Huger, Isaac, 58
Huger, Isaac, jun., 87
Huger, Isaac, sen., 87
Huger, John, 58, 96
Hughes, John, 12, 22
Hume, John, 55
Humphreys, Benjamin, 101
Hunt, ___, 82
Hunt, Mrs. ___, 101
Hunt, Thomas, 12
Hunter, Thomas, 82
Hunter, William, 22, 47
Hunter, E. & Jacob, 37
Hurst, Charles, 22
Hutchings, William, 61
Hutchings, William B., 62
Hutchinson, Jeremiah, 12
Hutchinson, John, 47
Hutchinson, Thomas, jun., 55
Hutchinson, Thomas, sen., 55
Hutson, Abel, 47
Hutson, Richard, 87, 107
Hutton, James, 96

Kelly, John, 37
Kelly, Mary, 48
Kelly, Tarence, 48
Kelsall, John, 101
Kelsey, John, 101
Kemmell, Mrs. ___, 101
Kemmell, Mary, 37
Kemmell, John, 12
Kempton, Ann, 37, 48
Kennan, Henry, 37
Kennear, Alexander, 37
Kennedy, Andrew, 37, 48
Kennedy, James, 56, 58
Kennedy, John, 37, 48
Kennedy, William, 48
Kennedy & Parker, 38
Kern, Frederick John, 38
Kern, John Frederick, 48
Kerr, Andrew, 38, 48
Kerr, John, 12, 22
Kersey, William, 38
Kershaw, Charles, 48
Kershaw, John, 12
Kershaw, Joseph, 22
Kershaw, William, 30
Kevan & Powrie, 38
Keyan, William, 48
King, Charles, 22
King, Eleanor, 38, 48
King, Timothy, 38
Kingman, Eliab, 22
Kingsley & Taylor, 30
Kinloch, Cleland, 56
Kinloch, Francis, 56
Kirk, John, 38
Kirk & Lukens, 48
Knight, Christopher, 76
Knoff, Conrad, 22
Know, Conrad, 12
Knox, Robert, 87
Kohne, John Frederick, 48
Kosskey, Anthony Jan, 12
Kraps, Andrew, 12
Kriebel, Frederick, 71
Kripps, Andrew, 48
Kruger, John Frederick, 71

Labbe, Anthony, 62
Ladson, Mrs. ___, 65
Ladson, James, 56, 90
Ladson, Jane, 97
Ladson, Sarah, 97
Lafar, Joseph, 62
Lafaver, Miss ___, 101
Lahisse, Maurice, 38
Lahogue, Feret, 101
Lamb, David, 107
Lamb & Montgomerie, 38
Lamb & Montgomery, 48
Lamotte, James, 48
LaMotte, James, 30, 38
Lamotte & Chisonn, 48
Lampe, John, 22
Lancaster, William, 12
Lance, Ann, 97, 101
Lance, Lambert, 76, 77
Lanchester, Henry, 38, 48
Lane, Alice, 97
Lane, Samuel, 22
Lang, Jane, 97
Lange, J. H., 48
Langford, Ann, 97, 101
Langstaff, John, 38, 48
Lanneau, Brazill, 23
Larabert, Frederick, 23
Larrey, Robert, 12
Larry, Robert, 23
Latham, Daniel, 12, 23
Latham, Eleanor, 61
Lathauson & co., 48
Lathrop & Snowdon, 107
Laughton, Winborn, 58
Laval, Jacint, 62
Lawrence, Estel, 12
Lawry, John, 38
Lawson & Price, 30, 107
Lawton, Winmal, 56
Lazarus, Mark, 38, 48
Lebbey, Nathaniel, 13
Leblanc, Henry, 23
Lechmere, Anthony, 30
Lee, Francis, 38
Lee, John & William, 48
Lee, Stephen, 13, 48
Lee, Thomas, 76, 77
Lee, William, 13, 23

Lee & Banks, 38
Lee & Miles, 48
Legare, Benjamin, 87
Legare, Daniel, 56
Legare, Daniel, jun., 56
Legare, Elizabeth, 101
Legare, Frances, 101
Legare, Samuel, 30, 38, 48, 107
Legare, Solomon, 38, 48
Legare, Thomas, 56, 58
Legare & Theus, 38
Legare, Theus, & Prioleau, 48
Legge, Edward, 56, 74
Legge, James, 48
Legge, Samuel, 13
Lehre, Mary, 97
Lehre, Thomas, 56, 58, 90
Lehre, William, 72
Lenneau, Bazil, 13
Lennox, William, 97
Lenox, William & co., 48
Lenud, Henry, 56
Lepoole, Peter, 38
Lesesne, Mrs. ___, 101
Lesesne, Isaac, 56
Lesesne, Sarah, 97
Leslie, George, 38
Leslie & Campbell, 48
Lesterjette & Cochran, 107
Levaux, John, 13
Levoux, John, 23
Levi, Hiram, 38
Levi, Moses, 38
Levi, Solomon, 38
Levy, Hart, 48
Levy, Lyon, 48
Levy, Moses C., 48
Levy, Nathan, 48
Levy, Samuel, 48
Levy, Solomon, 48
Lewers, Thomas, 48
Lewie & Coulback, 13
Lewis, Henry, 23
Ley, Francis, 48, 107
Libby, Nathaniel, 23
Liber, John, 13
Liblong, Henry, 13
Liddle, John, 48
Liedenhall, Johannas, 101

Lightwood, Edward, 30, 56, 58
Limehouse, Robert, 48
Limehouse, Thomas, 38
Lindsay, Robert, 38, 48
Lindsay, Robert & William, 31, 107
Linguard, Mary, 97, 102
Lining, Charles, 87
Linning, Charles, 90
Little, Robert, 13, 23
Littlejohn, Duncan, 48
Livingston, Eleanor, 102
Livingston, William, 97
Lloyd, John, 56, 58
Lloyd, John, jun., 38
Lloyd, Joseph, 38, 49
Lloyd & Paterson, 49
Lockey, Bradford and Co., 107
Lockey, George, 38
Lockwood, Joshua, 7, 38, 102
Lockwood, Thomas, 56
Logan, George, 87
Logan, Dr. George, 70
Logan, Mrs. George, 102
Logan, William, 38, 58
Long, Edward, 13
Long, Elizabeth, 97
Long, Lewis, 13
Loocock, Aaron, 56
Loocock, Mrs. Aaron, 102
Lopez, Aaron, 97
Lopez, David & Aaron, 74
Lord, Mrs. Andrew, 102
Lord, Ann, 97
Lord, Richard, 102
Lorimer, Alexander, 31
Lothrop, Seth, 38
Lothrop, Seth & co., 49
Love, John, 38, 49
Loveday, John, 38, 49
Lowndes, Rawlins, 56, 58, 93
Luckie, John, 13, 23
Lunt, Mary, 23
Lunt, William, 13
Luyton, William, 38, 49
Lynah, James, 71, 72
Lynch, James, 13
Lyon, Abraham, 13
Lyon, Mordecai, 13, 49
Lyon, Moses, 49

M'Arthur, John, 13
Macauley, George, 49
M'Beath, Alexander, 49
M'Beath & Ross, 49
Macbeth, Alexander, 31
M'Bride, James, 38, 49
M'Bride, Thomas, 38
M'Bride & Forsyth, 49
M'Call, Hext, 76
M'Call, James, 58, 87
M'Call, John, 13, 23, 31, 87, 90
M'Calla, Thomas, 71
M'Calla, Thomas H., 72
M'Callister, Archibald, 56
M'Callister, John, 13
M'Callum, James, 38
M'Callum & Ewing, 31, 107
M'Cann, Edward, 65
M'Carty, William, 90
M'Caully & Davis, 38
M'Caulay & Davis, 107
M'Clary, Jane, 65
M'Clish, Mrs. ___, 65
M'Clish, Alexander, 23
M'Clure, Cochran & W., 38, 49
M'Clure, Cochran and Wiliam, 108
M'Comb, James, 74
M'Connell, William, 13
M'Corkel, Samuel, 13
M'Cormick, Sparks & Co., 39
M'Crady, Edward, 38
M'Credie, David, 38
M'Credie, David & co., 49
M'Credie & Hamilton, 108
M'Donald, Archibald, 13
M'Donald, Charles, 39
M'Donald, Patrick, 49
M'Donald, William, 39, 49
M'Douall, James, 31
M'Dowall, James, 49
M'Dowall, John, 39, 49
M'Gee, John, 39, 49
M'Hugo, Anthony, 39
M'Intosh, Simon, 76, 77
M'Iver, John, 13, 23
MacIver, John & Alexander, 31
M'Kann, James, 64
M'Kee, Samuel, 39
M'Kenny, George, 23

M'Kenzie, Alexander, 39
M'Kenzie, Andrew, 39, 49
Mackenzie, Andrew & Co., 31
M'Kenzie, John, 80, 82
M'Kenzie, Kennedy, 13
M'Kenzie & Hinson, 49
Mackey, Crafts, 23
M'Khugo, Anthony, 90
Mackie, Ann, 97
Mackie, James, 13
Mackie & Williams, 23
M'Kimmy, John, 13, 23
M'Kimmy, William, 13
M'Kimmy, Mackie & Cameron, 7
M'Kinnon, Capt. ___, 86
M'Koy, Abraham F., 68
M'Lane, John, 88
M'Laren, James, 49
M'Lauchlan, Colin, 31
M'Lean, Evan, 13, 23
M'Lean, Lachlan, 13
M'Leish, Agnes, 39
M'Lellan & Wallace, 31
M'Leod, Angus, 108
Macleod, William, 49
M'Leod, William & Co., 108
M'Leod, Wm. and Co., 39
M'Lish, Mary, 61
M'Mahan, John, 39
M'Mullen, Richard, 23,
M'Murray, James & Co., 31
M'Nab, Alexander, 13
M'Nair & Maxwell, 31
M'Neal, Archibald, 39
M'Neale, Ralph, 8
M'Neil, Archibald, 13
M'Neil, Catharine, 39
Macomb, James, 74
M'Pherson, Duncan, 39, 49
M'Pherson, Jane, 39
M'Pherson, John, 56, 58
M'Queen, John, 39, 49
M'Queen, Robert, 39
M'Whann, William, 31, 39, 49, 108
Maden & Woodworth, 23
Magan, Patrick, 23
Magood, Simon, 97
Mailone, James, 49
Main, Thomas, 13

Miller, Rence, 97
Miller, Samuel, 14
Miller, William, 23
Miller & Robinson, 49
Milligan, Jacob, 88, 90
Milligan, James, 88, 90
Milligan, John, 50, 80, 82, 88
Milligan, Joseph, 23
Milligan and M'Kune, 14
Millin, John, 102
Milling & Oliver, 7
Mills, Rev. Mr. ___, 68
Mills, George, 14
Mills, William, 14, 23
Mills & Hicks, 7, 31
Milner, Daniel, 14, 23
Milner, George, 14, 23
Milner, John, 14
Minchin, John, 39
Minizing, Philip, 23
Minnick, John, 39, 50
Minott, John, 39
Minott, William, 81, 82
Mintsing, Christian, 14
Miott, Mrs. ___, 102
Miott, John, 14, 23
Mitchell, Andrew, 39, 50
Mitchell, Elizabeth, 97
Mitchell, Florine, 23
Mitchell, James, 102
Mitchell, John, 56, 88, 90, 87
Mitchell, John Hinckley, 50
Mitchell, Lazarus, 81
Mitchell, Mary, 97
Mitchell, William, 14
Mitchell, William, Boone, 77
Mitchell, Wm. Boone, 76
Mitchell & Donnom, 108
Moer, William, 14
Moncrieff, John, 14, 81
Moncrieff, John & Co., 39
Moncrieffe, Lt. Col. ___, 86
Montgomery, Thomas, 50
Mood, Peter, 14, 24
Moodie, Benjamin, 39, 90
Moore, John, 14, 24, 39, 50, 56, 82, 90
Moore, Joseph, 24, 39
Moore, Joseph Pitt, 72

Moore, Peter Joseph, 71
Moore, Philip, 24
Moore, Richard, 14
Moore, Thomas, 14
Moore and Denny, 14
Morgan, Ann, 97
Morgan, Charles, 7, 14, 24, 31, 108
Morgan, Edward, 88
Morris, George, 14
Morris, Mrs. George, 102
Morris, John, 73
Morris, Lewis, 56, 58
Morris, Mary, 97
Morris, Thomas, 39, 50, 88, 108
Morrison, Major ___, 86
Morrison, Ann, 14
Morrower, Margaret, 97
Mortimore, John, 24
Morton, William, 24
Moses, Abraham, 39
Moses, Abraham & H., 50
Moses, Barnet, 97
Moses, Henry, 40, 50
Moses, Isaac, 40, 50
Moses, Lyon, 40, 50
Moses, Philip, 50, 71, 72
Mota, Isaac, 50
Motte, Abraham, 40, 58
Motte, Francis, 40, 50
Motte, Isaac, 88, 90
Motter, Isaac, 97
Mouat, Mrs. John, 102
Moubray, William, 64
Moultrie, Alexander, 88, 90
Moultrie, James, 71, 72
Moultrie, William, 56, 90
Mowatt, George & Co., 31
Mucklehany, James, 82
Muir & Boyd, 50
Muirhead, James, 14, 24
Muller, Albert Arney, 88
Muller, Magdalen, 102
Mulligan, Francis, 40, 102
Munary, Robert, 14
Muncreef, Richard, 56
Muncreef, Susannah, 97
Muncrieff, John, 24
Muncrieff, John & co., 50
Muncrieff, Mary, 102

Parker, Isaac, 56
Parker, John, 24, 56, 58
Parker, John, jun., 77
Parker, John & George, 14
Parker, John & William, 108
Parker, Joseph, 14
Parker, Samuel, 102
Parker, Sarah, 102
Parker, Thomas, 77, 78
Parker, Wm. M'Kenzie, 78
Parker & Co., 31
Parkinson, John, 7, 14, 24
Parks, John, 24
Parrie, Murraline, 14
Parris, Francis, 50
Parsons, Susannah, 97, 102
Patrick, Casimer, 40
Patricks, Cashmere, 50
Patterson, William, 7, 14, 24
Patton, Alexander, 50
Patton, Catharine, 71, 72
Patton, Robert, 31
Paul, Andrew, 40
Payne, William, 40, 50
Payton, Richard Henry, 78
Peace, Isaac, 40, 50, 88
Peace, Isaac & Co., 108
Peace, Joseph, 78
Peak, John, 14
Pearce, Abraham, 31
Pearce, Mrs. Robert, 102
Pearse, John, 24
Peckham, Benjamin, 40
Pecton, Ruth, 61
Peebles, James, 24
Peignea, Lewis, 24
Peirson, James, 50
Pellason, Guilliam, 24
Pelsberry, Samuel, 90
Pelton, Roderick, 14
Pemble, Daivd, 14
Pencil, Emanuel, 15
Pencill, Emanuel, 24
Pendarvis, Josiah, 58
Penman, J. & E. & co., 50
Penman, James Ed. &, 40
Penman, James & Edward, 31, 108
Pepoon, Otis & co., 50
Peppin, Joseph & Co., 40, 50

Peppin, Matthew, 40
Peronneau, Henry, 93
Peronneau, Mary, 102
Peronneau, Dr. Robert, 70
Peronneau, William, 59
Perry, Edward, 59
Perry, Eleanor, 64
Pestch, Adam, 72
Peter, Henry, 50
Petrie, Edmund, 59
Petrie, Elizabeth, 97, 102
Petry, Monsieur ___, 88
Petsch, Adam, 71, 97
Phepoe, Thomas, 76
Philp, Robert, 93
Philips, Benjamin, 40
Philips, Benjamin, jun., 50
Philips, John C., 24
Philips, John Christian, 15
Philips, Thomas, 15
Pickens, Ezekiel, 78
Pierce, Benjamin, 15
Pierce, Robert, 15
Pillason, William, 64
Pilsbury, Samuel, 88
Pinckney, Charles, 59, 88, 93
Pinckney, Charles C., 78
Pinckney, Chas. C., 77
Pinckney, Frances, 97
Pinckney, Frances S., 98, 102
Pinckney, Thomas, 59
Pinckney, Thomas, jun., 56
Pinger, Lewis, 15
Piott, Peter, 24
Pitts, Frances, 98
Pleym, Andrew, 108
Plumb, Jacob, 15, 24
Plunkett, Thomas, 40
Poinsett, Elisha, 71
Poinsett, Dr. Elisha, 7
Pointset, Elisha, 72
Pollock, Solomon, 40, 55
Pope, Alexander, 15
Pope, Samuel, 15
Porcher, Philip, 56, 59
Porter, John, 108
Post office, 86, 102
Postell, Susannah, 10
Postell, Thomas, 56, 59

Rester, Henry, 40
Revel, John, 59
Revell, John, 83
Reyley, John, 15, 25
Reynolds, George, 15, 25
Rhind, Elizabeth, 61
Rhodes, John, 108
Rice, Thomas, 81
Richards, Gasper, 15, 25
Richardson, Barney, 25
Richardson, James, 59
Richardson, John, 31, 40, 51, 56
Richardson, John, jun., 31
Richon, Daivd, 25
Ridfield, Christopher, 15
Righton, Joseph, 15, 25
Righton, M'Cully, 15, 25
Rimeli, Martin, 15
Ripley, Paul, 81
Risk, Hugh & Co., 73
Rivers, Beulah, 25, 98
Rivers, Francis, 15, 59
Rivers, James, 25
Rivers, John, 56
Rivers, Samuel, 15, 25
Rivers, Thomas, 15, 25, 56
Roach, William, 103, 108
Robb, Michael, 25
Roberts, Ann, 98, 103
Roberts, John, 25
Roberts, Thomas, 15, 108
Roberts, William, 15, 25, 40, 51
Robertson, Alexander, 40, 51
Robertson, James, 7, 51
Robertson, John, 64, 88
Robertson, William, 78
Robinett, Francis, 25
Robinson, John, 15, 25
Robinson, Joseph, 15, 25
Robinson, William, 40, 51
Roche, Jeremiah, 40
Rodamond, Rachel, 98
Rogers, Christopher, 15, 25
Rogers, Lewis, 41, 51
Rogers, Maria, 61
Rogers, Sarah, 41, 51
Roggaman, Anthony, 15
Rogley, Anthony, 41
Rolander, Henry, 83

Rolinbury, Francis, 15
Roper, Hannah, 103
Roper, Joseph, 15, 25
Roper, Thomas, 56, 90
Roper, William, 93
Rosanbohm, Francis, 25
Rose, Alexander, 31, 51, 56
Rose, Hugh, 59
Rose, Dr. Hugh, 70
Rose, Jeremiah, 16
Rose, John, 93
Rose, Rebecca, 98
Ross, Alexander, 103
Ross, Elizabeth, 41, 51
Ross, George, 16
Ross, Kenneth, 41, 51
Ross, Malcolm, 16
Ross, Thomas, 81, 83
Ross, William-Kerr, 31
Roston, Lewis, 25
Roupel, Daniel, 16
Roupell, Daniel, 25
Roupell, George, 86, 103
Rouse, James, 16
Rouse, William, 16, 25
Rousseau, Peter, 25
Rout, George, 61, 62
Rout, Michael, 16
Rowand, Robert, 31, 51, 98
Rowe, Michael, 25
Royall, William, 61, 62
Ruberry, John, 16, 25
Rumney, Joseph, 16, 51
Rush, Mathias, 25
Rush, Matthias, 16
Russel, John & William, 8
Russel, William, 73
Russell, Ann, 98
Russell, Benjamin, 16, 25
Russell, George, 25
Russell, Jenkins & Co., 108
Russell, John, 25
Russell, Mary, 103
Russell, Nathaniel, 41, 51
Russell, Commander Thomas, 108
Rutledge, Edward, 77, 78, 108
Rutledge, Edward, jun., 78
Rutledge, Hugh, 77, 90, 108
Rutledge, John, 90, 108

Simmons, Francis, 57
Simmons, Thomas, 57
Simmons, William, 26, 57
Simmons, Vanderhorst & co., 51
Simons, Anthony, 41
Simons, Francis, 66
Simons, James, 57
Simons, Keating, 51, 91
Simons, Maurice, 31
Simons, Sampson, 98
Simons, Samuel, 41, 103
Simons, Thomas, 51, 57
Simons, Blake & Vanderhorst, 41
Simpson, John & Thomas, 31
Simpson, John & William, 109
Simpson, Jonathan & William, 31
Simpson, Mary, 16
Singleton, Bracey, 64
Singleton, Daniel, 16
Singleton, Richard, 59
Singleton, Thomas, 91, 98
Sinkler, James, 57
Siser, Michael, 16
Sisley, Lewis, 16
Skene, Dr. James, 70
Skirving, Charlotte, 98, 103
Skirving, William, 57, 59
Skottowe, Thomas, 86
Skrine, William, 41, 103
Slann & Guignard, 109
Slowman, Henry, 16
Slowman, John, 16
Smerdon, Elias, 41
Smerdon, Henry, 109
Smiser, Hannah, 103
Smith, Mrs. ___, 66, 103
Smith, Andrew, 41
Smith, Archibald, 41, 51
Smith, Caleb, 51
Smith, Christiana, 62
Smith, Daniel, 98, 103
Smith, Desaussure & Darrel, 41
Smith, George, 41
Smith, James, 41, 51, 77, 78
Smith, John, 16, 32, 41, 57, 81
Smith, John, jun., 32
Smith, John & Archibald, 109
Smith, John Christian, 51
Smith, John Holmes, 51

Smith, John Press, 71
Smith, Josiah, 41, 103
Smith, Julius, 32, 51
Smith, Morton, 64, 91
Smith, Nicholas, 8
Smith, O'Brian, 59
Smith, Obrien, 57
Smith, Peter, 16, 26, 57, 59
Smith, Richard, 103
Smith, Rev. Robert, 68
Smith, Rev. Dr. Robert, 68
Smith, Roger, 32, 41, 59
Smith, Roger & Peter, 109
Smith, Samuel, 16, 26, 41, 103
Smith, Solomon, 8
Smith, Thomas, 57, 81, 83
Smith, Mrs. Thomas, 103
Smith, Thomas Rhett, 78
Smith, Whiteford, 41
Smith, Whitford, 51
Smith, William, 26, 32, 41, 51
Smith, Rev. William, 61, 68
Smith, William & Co., 109
Smiths, Desaussure & Darrell, 109
Smyser, Hannah, 98
Smyth, John, 32, 52, 98
Smyth, Roger, 41, 59
Snead, James, 8
Snipes, William Clay, 57
Snitter, Charles, 16, 26
Snodgrass, William, 32
Snowden, Charles, 41, 52
Snyder, Paul, 16
Solomons, Hyam, 52
Somersall, Thomas A., 52
Somersall, William, 32, 41, 52
Somersall, Wm. & son, 52
Somervill & Duguid, 32
Sommers, John, 16
Sommers, Martha, 98
Spaving, Patrick, 41
Spears, James, 16, 26
Speisegger, John, jun., 41
Spencer, George, 41
Spencer, Sebastian, 16
Spering, Patrick, 52
Spiddle, Elizabeth, 103
Spidle, George, 16
Spiessager, John, 26

Tew, Charles, 42, 103
Tew, John, 26
Tew, Thomas, 17
Thayer, Bartlett & Co., 42
Thayer, Ebenezer, 52
Thayer, William and J., 52
Thayer & Bartlet, 109
Therie, John Francis, 52
Theus, James, 42, 52, 91
Theus, Rosanna, 65, 103
Theus, Samuel, 52
Theus, Simeon, 57, 103
Thomas, Elizabeth, 66
Thomas, Francis, 52
Thomas, James, 52
Thomas, John, 17, 26
Thomas, John B., 42
Thomas, John David, 52
Thomas, Mary Lamboll, 98, 103
Thomas, Stephen, 17, 26
Thompson, Daniel, 42
Thompson, Esther, 42
Thompson, J. Hamden, 61
Thompson, James, 17
Thompson, John, 62, 81
Thompson, John & William, 32
Thompson, Peter, 17
Thompson & Lennox, 109
Thomson, Archibald, 83
Thomson, Daniel, 52
Thomson, Elizabeth, 66
Thomson, George, jun., 32
Thomson, James H., 62
Thomson, Jane, 8
Thomson, John, 59, 81, 83
Thorn, John, 17
Thorn, John G., 26
Thorne, Philip, 64
Threadcraft, Bethel, 17, 26
Timmons, Lewis, 74
Timothy, Ann, 88, 109
Timothy, Benjamin F., 26
Timothy & Mason, 91
Tobias, Joseph, 42, 52
Todd, John, 57, 65
Todd, Joseph, 42
Tonge, Mark, 42, 52
Tool, Michael, 26
Toole, John, 17

Toole, Michael, 17
Toomer, Anthony, 17, 26
Torrance, William H., 78
Torry, Elias, 81
Toussiger, James, 17
Tragg, Lawrence, 17
Traile, Major ___, 86
Trenas, George, 17
Trenholm, William, 42, 52
Trescot, Edward, 88, 91, 109
Trezevant, Lewis, 78
Trezevant, Peter, 42, 52
Trezevant, Theodore, 17, 26
Troup, John, 76, 77, 78
Tucker, Benjamin, 81, 83
Tucker, Mary, 62
Tufts & Ryan, 32
Tullock, Peter, 52
Tunno, Adam, 52, 109
Tunno, Adam & Willm., 42
Tunno, George, 42
Tunno, John & Adam, 32
Tunno, Thomas, 52
Tunno, William, 52
Tunnos & Cox, 52
Turnbull, Andrew, 71
Turnbull, Dr. Andrew, 70
Turner, David Watson, 91
Turner, Shadrack, 81
Turner, Thomas, 62
Turpin, Hannah, 65, 66
Turpin, William, 42, 52
Tweed, Alexander, 57, 59
Tydeman, Mrs. ___, 103

Vacanna, ___, 26
Vale, John David, 42, 59
Valk, Jacob, 32
Vanassendelst, William, 83
Vanderhorst, Arnoldus, 59, 88
Van Rhyn & Newman, 109
Van Ryan & Savage, 52
Vanrynn, Emelina, 42
Vansilver, ___, 72
Vardell, Elizabth, 98, 103
Vardell, Robert, 17, 26

Velsing, John, 17
Ver Cnocke, F. I., 42
Vercnocke & Cockle, 52
Veree, Joseph, 42, 52, 103
Veree, Mary, 98
Vesier, M., 103
Veyong, George, 17
Villepontoux, Benj., 42
Villepontoux, Jane, 103
Villepontoux & Co., 109
Villeret, Mary, 103
Vinyard, John, 8
Virgin, George, 42, 52
Vliex, Frederick, 26
Vos, Andrew, 42, 52
Vos & Graves, 53

Wadsworth & Porter, 109
Wadsworth & Turpin, 53
Wagner, Christopher, 17, 26
Wagner, George, 53, 98
Wagner, John, 32, 42, 59
Wainwright, Richard, 57, 59
Wakefield, James, 109
Walcot, Samuel, 42
Waldren, Samuel, 81
Walker, Alexander, 109
Walker, Robert, 17
Walker, Sylvanus, 88
Walker & Maitland, 32, 109
Walkman, Mark, 42
Wall, Richard Gilbert, 53
Wallace, Elizabeth, 65
Wallace, James, 42
Wallace, Thomas, 17
Wallis, Hugh, 26
Wallis, James, 91
Wallis, Thomas, 27
Wallis, William, 27
Walters, William, 17
Ward, John, 77, 78
Ward, Joshua, 76, 77, 78
Ward, Love, 98, 103
Ward, Samuel, 109
Ward, Theonhilus, 62
Warham, Charles, 42, 59
Waring, John, 59

Waring, Joseph, 57
Waring, Mary, 103
Waring, Thomas, 42, 53, 88
Warley, Elizabeth, 103
Warley, Felix, 91
Warl;ey, Foelix, 88
Warley, George, 17
Warnock, Joseph, 66
Warrington, James, 32
Warrington, Nicholas, 8
Warson, Thomas, 27
Warwick, Anthony & Co., 32
Washing, Gasper, 17
Washing, John, 17
Washington, William, 57, 59
Waties, Thomas, 88, 91
Watson, Alexadner, 42, 53
Watson, Isaac, 53
Watson, John, 17, 27
Watson, John & George, 17
Watson, Joseph, 27
Watson & Dennison, 73
Watts, Charles, 17, 27
Watts, John, 17
Wayne, Richard, 32
Wayne, Sarah, 17
Weare, Peter, 17
Weaver, Peter, 27
Webb, John, 42, 53
Webb, William, 99
Webb & Doughty, 109
Webster, Thomas, 81, 83
Welch, George, 18, 53
Welch, John, 88, 91
Welch, Mary, 66
Welch, Thomas, 27
Wells, Edgar, 42
Wells, Edgar & son, 53
Wells, R. & Son, 8, 32
Wells, Richard, 103
Wells & Bethune, 109
Wershing, John, 27
Wesner, Philip, 103
Wesner, Philip Henry, 65
Wessinger, John, 27
West, Thomas Wade, 104
Westermyer, Andrew, 27
Westermyer, Henry, 18
Weston, John Holybush, 78